Plantations and Historic Homes of South Carolina

Jai Williams

Globe Pequot

Guilford, Connecticut

Globe
Pequot

An imprint of The Rowman & Littlefield Publishing Group, Inc.

4501 Forbes Blvd., Ste. 200
Lanham, MD 20706
www.rowman.com

Distributed by NATIONAL BOOK NETWORK

Copyright © 2019 Jai Williams

Photography by Jai Williams

British Library Cataloguing in Publication Information available

Library of Congress Cataloging-in-Publication Data available

ISBN 978-1-4930-3601-1 (hardcover)

ISBN 978-1-4930-3602-8 (e-book)

∞™ The paper used in this publication meets the minimum requirements of American National Standard for Information Sciences—Permanence of Paper for Printed Library Materials, ANSI/NISO Z39.48-1992

Printed in the United States of America

To the women in my life who are a continuous source of inspiration, love, and support; thank you.

Contents

Acknowledgments

"Appreciation is a wonderful thing. It makes what is excellent in others belong to us as well."

VOLTAIRE

I would like to sincerely thank the many people who contributed to this project. To the executive directors, who gave permission to visit as well as photograph each plantation and/or historic home; to the docents, who contributed enthusiastic interpretations during tours; and to the historians as well as curators, who provided feedback to make sure each essay was historically factual.

To Jayson Sellers of Hampton Plantation, Elizabeth Laney of Redcliffe Plantation, Shawn Halifax of McLeod Plantation, Lucy Archie of Drayton Hall, and Jeff Neale of Middleton Place, who, without pretense, desire to diligently discuss the horrors of slavery as well as shine light on the African-American families who were enslaved for generations at these sites.

To Don Bussey of Middleton Place, Jennifer McCormick of The Charleston Museum, Jordan Bannister of Historic Pendleton, Halie Brazier of Historic Camden, Lauren Northup of the Historic Charleston Foundation, Anna Kate Twitty of Historic Columbia, and Marie Cheek of Historic Brattonsville, whose dedication to these architectural masterpieces is unmatched.

To Nate and Stephanie of Rose Hill, your kindness was refreshing. To Trenda, Nathan, and Andrew, I look forward to supporting each of your future endeavors; your brilliance is inspiring.

Last but not least, to Reina, Jane, Raven, and Stephanie, thank you for providing a safe space in a place unknown.

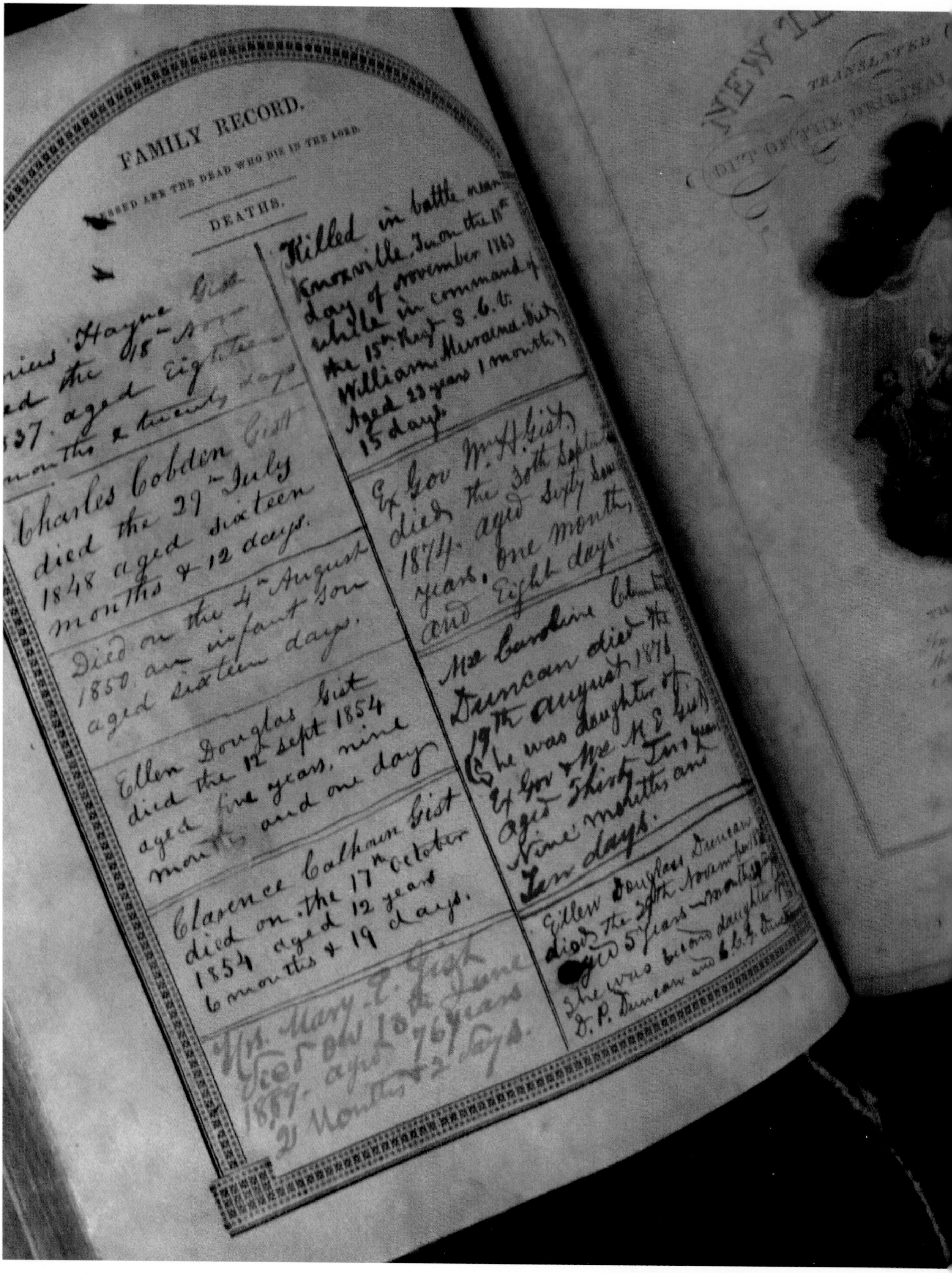

FAMILY RECORD.

[BLES]SED ARE THE DEAD WHO DIE IN THE LORD.

DEATHS.

[...rius] Hayne Gist
[di]ed the 18th Nov—
[18]37. aged Eighteen
[m]onths & twenty days

Killed in battle near
Knoxville. Tenn on the 15th
day of November 1863
while in command of
the 15th Regt. S.C.V.
William Muraine Gist
Aged 23 years 1 month &
15 days.

Charles Cobden Gist
died the 27th July
1848 aged sixteen
months & 12 days.

Died on the 4th August
1850. an infant Son
aged sixteen days.

Ex Gov Wm H. Gist
died the 30th Septr
1874. aged Sixty Seven
years, one month,
and Eight days.

Ellen Douglas Gist
died the 12 Sept 1854
aged five years, nine
months, and one day

Mrs Caroline Clendinin
Duncan died the
19th August 1876
She was daughter of
Ex Gov & Mrs W E Gist
aged Thirty Two years
Nine months and
Ten days.

Clarence Calhoun Gist
died on the 17th October
1854 aged 12 years
6 months & 19 days.

Ellen Douglas Duncan
died the 30th November 1876
Aged 5 years—months
She was second daughter of
G. P. Duncan and E. G. G. Duncan

Mrs. Mary E. Gist
died the 10th June
1887— aged 76 years
2 Months & 2 days.

Introduction

It is a matter of common knowledge that the government of South Carolina is under domination of a small ring of cunning, conniving men.

STROM THURMOND

South Carolina, also known as the Palmetto State, is located along the Eastern Seaboard of the United States, which runs from Maine to Florida. In 1663 King Charles II granted a charter to eight men of nobility referred to as Lord Proprietors. Men such as Sir William Berkeley; Edward Hyde, First Earl of Clarendon; and Anthony Ashley Cooper, First Earl of Shaftesbury, dispersed large amounts of land to English settlers who desired to and could afford to expand into unsoiled territories of the New World. In 1670 colonists landed along the Ashley River establishing the first permanent settlement in the province of Carolina. The settlement subsequently moved to the intersecting point of the Ashley and Cooper Rivers, where it remains today.

Due to the mismanagement of colonial affairs, the province split into northern and southern territories in 1712; however, the proprietors still officially controlled both areas. In 1719 colonists rebelled against proprietary rule, appealing to the crown for intervention. Redemption was slow, as it took ten years for the crown to completely intervene, buying seven of the eight proprietors' land back. Both North and South Carolina shifted from being proprietary colonies to royal colonies beginning in 1729 and staying so until the American Revolution. On May 23, 1788, South Carolina received its statehood and remained a part of the United States until it seceded on December 20, 1860. Eight years later, in 1868, South Carolina was readmitted into the Union.

Since its inception as a colony, South Carolina always boasted a strong agricultural presence due to its early exportation of goods such as tobacco and later indigo, yet the introduction of rice and enslaved people from Africa to its coastline in 1685 significantly changed everything. Referenced as Carolina Gold, the rice industry became South Carolina's main commercial crop by the early eighteenth century and remained so until the late nineteenth century when rice production shifted to other southern states such as Louisiana and Texas. Nonetheless, the amount of capital that had been acquired by rice farmers provided wealth for generations to come. Their acquisition led to massive plantations and immaculate homes built throughout the colony and thereafter the state, some still standing today. We've compiled a collection of over thirty houses spanning over two centuries of history for you to explore, experience, and visit when you're in the Palmetto State.

Every good citizen makes his country's honor his own, and cherishes it not only as precious but as sacred. He is willing to risk his life in its defense and is conscious that he gains protection while he gives it.

ANDREW JACKSON

As the tenth colony of the original thirteen, the province of Carolina saw its share of territorial wars commencing with Queen Anne's War (1702–1713), then shortly thereafter, the Yamasee War (1715–1717), followed decades later by the Cherokee (Anglo-Cherokee) War (1759–1761). During

Queen Anne's War Great Britain sought to halt France's expansion within North America as well as secure and protect British colonists living along the New England frontier and within Charleston from French forces. Although at opposite ends of the continent, France occupied both the Nova Scotia territory of Port-Royal and the lower Mississippi valley.

Two years later tensions between the Yamasee Indians and the colonists came to a head. The Yamasee Indians, along with members from other tribes, fought fiercely against the English settlers' aggressive acquisition of land and encroachment on well-established Indian trading routes. The war was costly for the Indians, as the colonists eventually won and the Yamasees' land and power was diminished in the southeastern region of the colony. Brutal treatment by the English toward the Cherokee also led to hostility and violence

between the two groups, ending similarly with the Cherokees losing much of their bountiful hunting grounds. Relations would remain strained between the colonists and various tribes for decades to come.

By the time of the Revolutionary War (1775–1783), the colonists had a systematic plan in place to secure the colonies' independence and form the United States of America. What perhaps is not known, is that South Carolina had more than 200 battles occur on its soil during the American Revolution. At its end, war ceased for almost a century until the American Civil War broke out during

the Battle of Fort Sumter on April 12, 1861. Most of the families mentioned throughout this book had members who fought in one or more of the aforementioned wars.

LEGACY FAMILIES

There never has yet existed a wealthy and civilized society in which one portion of the community did not, in point of fact, live on the labor of the other.

JOHN C. CALHOUN

What's in a name? It depends on whom you ask. For the founding families of Charleston and its surrounding area, a last name provides a subtle acknowledgment of one's ancestors and their accomplishments in the development of the southern colony. As Scottish, Irish, and other immigrant groups arrived here in the eighteenth and nineteenth centuries, it became an important distinction. Names such as Alston, Boone, Colleton, Drayton, Gibbes, Horry, Huger, Legare, Manigault, Middleton, Pinckney, Ravenel, and Serre can be found on municipal buildings and spaces throughout the city. Descendants of many of these families still live in the original homes such as the Edmondston-Alston House. A select few of these homes have remained in the same family since they were built. At least three of those home's stories are within these pages: Drayton Hall, Magnolia Plantation, and Middleton Place.

Why do families stay? While some descendants choose to directly partake in their ancestral home's daily interaction, others realize that the required time, upkeep, and commitment may be something they are willing to forgo. This has allowed national and nonprofit organizations such as the National Trust for Historic Preservation and the Middleton Foundation to enter the picture and protect and care for these snapshots of American history. Additionally, local preservation foundations have formed to keep the flame lit, including Historic Beaufort, Historic Columbia, Historic Charleston, Middleton Foundation, and others.

A question frequently asked is, "Do descendants of both the enslaved and namesake families come to visit?" The answer varies; for some places it is yes, for others no, as these spaces hold various memories for different people. Those who had full access to the riches and opportunities benefited greatly, while those who toiled to make that lifestyle possible suffered greatly. Interestingly over the years, members laying claim to a bloodline both black, white, and of mixed race have come together during family reunions to heal and help one another recognize the past, honor the present, and forge forward toward a candid future.

Until the silent majority takes over from the vocal minority, nothing in this state will change.

MODJESKA MONTEITH SIMKINS

An institution practiced since ancient times, slavery has been a point of contention for many nations. However, the Americas, particularly the South, have had an almost unshakable attachment to it, including the brutal treatment of four million slaves once present on its soil. The southern colonies of Virginia, Maryland, North and South Carolina, and Georgia practiced either gang or task-system slavery. Gang slavery involved a repetitive action by a large group of slaves at once while the task system gave an enslaved person a specific task in which, upon completion, he or she was given a certain level of autonomy to engage in acts such as growing his or her own crops, going into town with permission, or simply resting. South Carolina adopted the latter system while other southern colonies adopted the former. Nonetheless, a question to consider is whether the tasks given were actually achievable in one day.

Once again it depended on if one was a slave or master, as those in control wanted to make sure that slaves were always working to their maximum capacity. The time it took for the same task to be accomplished could vary depending on age and gender. Meticulous notes were taken by a few of the owners, found in the families' papers. Because of their references a better idea has been provided of how slaves labored for almost the next for 300 years in South Carolina.

All of the homes and the plantations mentioned in this book participated in either rural or urban slavery at some point in their history. However, there are stories of survival and success out of these oppressive conditions. Take, for example, Mary Jane McLeod Bethune, who became a special advisor to an American president; Dr. Matilda Arabelle Evans, who became the first black woman in the state of South Carolina to practice medicine; and Viola Davis, the only African-American who has won the "Triple Crown of Acting," which consists of a Tony, an Oscar, and an Emmy. Yet most important to remember are those who remain nameless, whose stories are untold and may never be. Those who contributed to a cause greater than any award or recognition could ever provide . . . freedom.

Coastal Plains/Coastal Region

The ocean stirs the heart, inspires the imagination and brings eternal joy to the soul.

ROBERT WYLAND

South Carolina's coastal plains include both the outer and inner coastal regions with cities such as Charleston, Hilton Head Island, Conway, and Florence. The weather is usually hot and humid. This area also includes some of the most populous cities due to its numerous sandy beaches, islands, and rivers.

Aiken-Rhett House

48 Elizabeth St.
Charleston, SC 29403
historiccharleston.org

The Home of a Governor

The Aiken-Rhett House has survived for almost two centuries. Built circa 1820, the house stayed within the Aiken-Rhett family for more than 140 years. First owned by Charleston merchant John Robinson, the house was constructed in the Charleston double style, a favorite during the late eighteenth and early nineteenth centuries.

Due to financial obligations, Robinson sold the house to William Aiken Sr. in 1827. Born in 1779, Aiken emigrated from Ireland to the United States. Founding the South Carolina Canal and Rail Road Company, he would later serve as its president from 1828 to 1831. When Aiken died in a carriage accident, his assets transferred to his wife Henrietta and his only son, William Aiken Jr.

Born in 1806, William Jr. lived in Charleston, South Carolina, for his primary and secondary education. Pursuing a degree in agriculture at the College of South Carolina, he graduated in 1825. Eight years later, in 1833, William married Harriet Lowndes. Following his father's death in that same year, William Jr. and Harriet resided in this lavish residence. Like any young couple, they made updated renovations to the property showcasing their enormous wealth.

Operating a rice plantation on Jehossee Island, William Jr. continued to grow his holdings. The US Census of 1840 shows him owning twenty-one slaves; however, it is hard to tell if these enslaved people lived and worked only at his Charleston residence, as their rice plantation would have required a larger workforce. By the 1850s there were over five hundred enslaved people living and working on Jehossee Island.

William Jr. ran for governor and won in 1844, serving a single term until 1846. He was elected to the US House of Representatives, serving from 1851 until 1857. Subsequently, he and his wife left again to travel around Europe, something that was typical for the upper class during the nineteenth century to do to acquire various pieces of art and furniture for their homes. While abroad, William Jr. employed his cousin Joseph Daniel Aiken to create an art gallery. A novel idea for the time, the room still holds articles obtained by the Aikens during their European travels.

Once the Civil War approached, William Jr. was asked to choose a side, but decided to remain neutral. When he declined to attend a national-flag-raising ceremony over Fort Sumter after its surrender, he was arrested and sent to Washington, DC where he remained under guard. Appealing

to President Andrew Johnson, William Jr. was later released, as the two men were acquaintances from their days in Congress.

William Jr. died in 1887, leaving his property to his wife. She and their daughter Henrietta lived there until Harriet's death in 1892. As the Aikens' only daughter, Henrietta inherited her parents' wealth. Marrying Major Andrew Burnet Rhett, Henrietta had five children. Upon her death on December 14, 1918, the house was split among her heirs. Lived in by family members until the mid-twentieth century, the home was sold to The Charleston Museum in 1975. In 1995, the Historic Charleston Foundation purchased the property.

Today, a forty-five-minute, self-guided audio tour takes the public throughout three levels of the museum, including the slave quarters as well as stables located on the premises. The use of technology brings the nineteenth century into the twenty-first.

Boone Hall Plantation

1235 Long Point Rd.
Mt Pleasant, SC 29464
boonehallplantation.com

ONE OF AMERICA'S OLDEST WORKING FARMS

Boone Hall's history began with Major John Boone in 1681. Established on the banks of Wampacheone Creek, the plantation is one of the oldest working farms in America and recognizable by its live oak alley. Previously growing cotton and pecans, the plantation now offers peaches, strawberries, and other fruits and vegetables at the Boone Hall Farms Market, located two miles from the main house. Additionally, the market boasts an award-winning butcher shop and offers fresh seafood straight from the docks.

There's much to do while on the old plantation grounds, whether its touring the house built in 1936 by Canadian ambassador Thomas Stone or learning about the culture of the Gullah, an African-American population who are specific to the coastal region of the southeastern states, particularly South Carolina, Georgia, and Florida. There is also a "Black History in America" exhibit and a slave presentation. For those interested in Boone Hall's agricultural history, there is a plantation tractor tour, which covers the farm's entire 738 acres; a garden tour, which showcases antique roses over 100 years old; and a butterfly pavilion. From the rare and beautiful sweetgrass baskets available to purchase to numerous events held annually, Boone Hall Plantation offers something for everyone.

Drayton Hall

3380 Ashley River Rd.
Charleston, SC 29414
draytonhall.org

AN AMERICAN ICON

Twelve miles outside of Charleston, 350 acres of unspoiled land sat along the Ashley River. Answering a for-sale ad in the *South Carolina Gazette* in 1738, John Drayton purchased the land on which to build what would become his namesake. As the youngest son of Thomas Drayton and Ann Fox, he knew their ancestral house at what is today Magnolia Plantation would be passed along to his older brother Thomas Drayton so, at twenty-three, John bought the plot of land less than two miles from his parents' plantation. Unlike other house constructed during that period, his was opulent and designed to rival anything previously seen in that time.

It would take more than a decade to finish Drayton Hall, as no expense was spared. John employed a plethora of artisans, as well as enslaved African-Americans. Materials for construction

were gathered from the surrounding area, including a mixture of clay and water left behind from earlier rice cultivation from which bricklayers kilned 360,000 bricks to make up Drayton Hall's Flemish bond exterior. Additionally, limestone imported from England was used to construct the portico. Upon its completion, Drayton Hall became an exquisite example of Palladian architecture in the eighteenth century.

Drayton Hall was completed in 1750. Two years later John married his third wife, Margaret Glen. Once the two moved in, the property served more like a command post than a working farm. John owned 76,000 acres and more than 100 plantations in South Carolina. He cultivated crops such as indigo and rice. When Margaret died in 1772, John waited three years before marrying his fourth and final wife Rebecca Perry from a neighboring plantation. With more than a forty-year age difference between them, their union caused a bit of talk among the community.

When the Revolutionary War commenced in 1775, John and Rebecca vacated Drayton Hall accompanied by their young children. Unfortunately, as the Draytons crossed into safer territories, John died from a seizure in 1779. Rebecca never remarried and continued to control Drayton Hall's affairs, even protecting the property during the British occupation of her home in 1780 by Charles Cornwallis and Alexander Leslie. In 1784 Rebecca decided to move to Charleston and sold Drayton Hall to her stepson, Charles Drayton.

Considered the documentarian of the family, Charles kept a diary for more than thirty years, including the additional design changes he made to the house as well as details of his daily life. It is through his journal that we learn about the enslaved population at Drayton Hall; however, unfortunately, little is recorded except first names, titles, and tasks accomplished.

When Charles died in 1820, his son Dr. Charles Drayton II inherited the house, and it remained in family hands until sold to the National Trust for Historic Preservation in 1974. In 2015, the Drayton Hall Preservation Trust took over operations of Drayton Hall. The trust focuses on how the house was received from Drayton descendants, completely void of furniture. Without furnishings, it tells a story of the 235 years Drayton Hall remained in one family. The grounds surrounding the house include a privy, a caretaker's house that focuses on the African-American population in the postbellum period, an exhibit gallery, and an education center. Intertwining these various pieces of cultural interaction, the Drayton Hall Preservation Trust has created a place where the preservation of an American icon is at the forefront for generations to come.

Edmondston-Alston House

21 East Battery
Charleston, SC 29401
edmondstonalston.com

WATERFRONT REAL ESTATE

Born in Scotland, in 1782 Charles Edmondston sought and found a better life in Charleston. He made a name for himself as a prominent shipping merchant, exporting and importing goods. The plot of land he chose for his home once housed Fort Mechanic, named after the occupations of those who labored there. The fort was built in 1794 and abandoned in 1809. Edmondston purchased the land in 1817; he was thirty-five years old.

Before Charleston built its seawall in 1820, the inlet known as Charleston Harbor was uninhabitable. Once put into place, the seawall allowed the land to dry out, making it suitable for the construction of houses and buildings. Over the next century, various styles of architecture decorated the cityscape of the bustling seaport including examples of Colonial, Georgian, and Federal styles.

Edmondston chose to build his new home in the Federal style, displaying his wealth for all to see. It was completed in 1825 and he was able to enjoy it for almost ten years before the Panic of 1837 forced him to sell. Edmondston relinquished the property to Charles Cotesworth Alston in 1838.

Born in Georgetown, South Carolina, Alston came from a prosperous planter family who owned numerous plantations, including Fairfield, Clifton, and Strawberry Hill. His purchase of a city mansion allowed him and his family to leave the mosquito-infested rice fields and enjoy Charleston's social scene, especially during horse racing season. His father, William Alston, had assisted in creating the Fourth Carolina Jockey Club in 1792. Charles Alston enhanced the house, adding Greek Revival touches such as faux marble, decorated cornices, and an overall symmetrical shape. The house was also one of the first to be piped with gas.

When the first shots of the Civil War ricocheted from Fort Sumter, Charlestonians on the opposite side of the harbor realized they were in the direct line of fire. Leaving town in the spring of 1861, some abandoned their homes and whatever possessions they could not carry; however, it is believed that Susan Alston and her mother remained at their home until 1863. When the war ended, the federal government confiscated many empty homes them as rebel property, including Alston's. He appealed the decision, stating that his house had been occupied throughout the war. The federal government acquiesced, returning

the mansion to Alston. Today, more than 150 years later, the eighth generation of the Alston family lives upstairs on the third floor.

Present-day tours showcase historical artifacts, such as one of the remaining thirteen Ordinance of Secession framed in the parlor. Across the hallway, in the formal dining room, four pieces of silver smithed by Mrs. Hester Bateman during the eighteenth century shine brilliantly. Upstairs in the light-filled library, a rifle designed by famed James Purdey & Co. sits in a glass box. Both drawing rooms hold period furniture, but the west room displays rare Audubon prints. Sweeping views of the harbor are breathtaking from the home's second-floor balcony, mostly enjoyed during visiting hours. However, don't be discouraged, as behind the house sits 21 East Battery Bed & Breakfast, where guests can reside in luxurious accommodations while reveling in one of Charleston's beautiful sunsets.

The Ordinance of Secession

The State of South Carolina.

Frampton Plantation House

1 Low Country Ln.
Yemassee, SC 29945
southcarolinalowcountry.com

HOLD THE LINE

Receiving a land grant from King George II, the Framptons were one of the first families to settle in the area. On February 22, 1709, John Frampton obtained a warrant for 500 acres of land in Colleton County. He continued to acquire land throughout the county over the next two years until he owned approximately 1,200 acres. The family's lineage split over the next century, and on December 30, 1810, John Edward Frampton was born in Beaufort County.

It is believed that John Edward's father, also John Frampton, built the family plantation house in 1840. Situated as it was on a hill, it became known as the Hill Plantation. The Framptons owned other plantations in the Low Country including Hermitage Plantation located in Varnville, a town in Hampton County where John Edward and his wife Harriet Hay may have lived after their marriage in 1841.

Although a planter, John Edward did not rest on his laurels and represented Prince William's Parish in the state senate from 1842 until 1845. In 1849, when his father died, John Edward inherited Hill Plantation.

Around this time, Prince William's Parish consisted of many wealthy Charleston planter families such as the Manigaults and Heywards. Located within the Ace Basin, the area was an ideal location to cultivate Sea Island cotton as well as Carolina Gold rice due to the estuaries flowing into the Combahee and Coosawhatchie Rivers.

By 1860, the US Census shows John Edward's real estate holdings at more than $50,000, while his net worth was valued at $100,000. That same year, the US Census Slave Schedule recorded him owning 131 slaves. Frampton as well as other planters in the area signed the Ordinance of

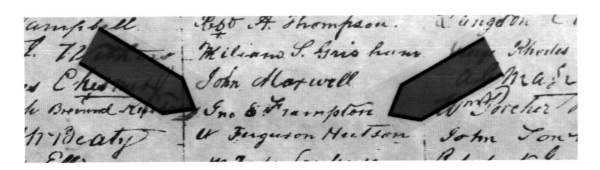

Secession in December of 1860. When the Civil War broke out, Frampton served as a delegate to the Secession Convention from Prince William's Parish. With such proximity to Charleston, southern families vacated the area as fighting intensified.

Confederate troops erected an intricate system of earthworks to protect the Charleston & Savannah Railroad. Built in 1854, the railroad traveled 120 miles between these two important coastal cities. Their strategic locations contributed to the need for their protection as they provided supplies and materials to the Confederacy. On October 21, 1862, thousands of Union troops arrived in Pocotaligo hoping to destroy the railroad. While waiting for reinforcements from General P.G.T. Beauregard, Colonel W.S. Walker of Georgia held off the advance with 450 men, thanks to the infrastructure conceived by General Robert E. Lee. Remnants of the system can still be seen behind the plantation.

During his Carolina Campaign, General William Sherman torched everything in sight, including Hill Plantation. John Edward rebuilt his farmhouse in 1868. Owned by the Frampton family until 1947, the house then changed hands numerous times, eventually falling into disrepair. Thankfully, in 1993, the Low Country Tourism Commission acquired and restored the building to its current condition.

Hampton Plantation

1950 Rutledge Rd.
McClellanville, SC 29458
southcarolinaparks.com/hampton

JUST AROUND THE RIVER BEND

Lived in by some of the most recognized families of the antebellum era, including the Horrys, Pinckneys, and Rutledges, Hampton Plantation is a diamond in the rough. Surrounded by abandoned rice fields, the former planation is situated along the South Santee River. Formerly known as the Rice Kingdom between 1730 and 1840, the Santee Delta contributed to making South Carolina the then-wealthiest colony among the British North American colonies.

Built between 1735 and 1750 by Noe Serre and his wife Catherine, the plantation came into the possession of Daniel Horry in 1757 through his marriage to Noe's and Catherine's daughter Judith. Eight years later Judith died and Daniel married Harriott Pinckney and had two children, Harriott and Daniel. The Horrys expanded their home from 5,000 square feet to 10,000 square feet and owned about twenty outbuildings that dotted the landscape. The entrance initially faced Hampton Creek, but just prior to President George Washington's visit to South Carolina in 1791, the Horrys built an Adamesque portico on the back of the house, essentially making it the front entrance. Cypress timbers and heart pine floors make up the Georgian-style home. The symmetrical design of the house was typical for the period.

Inside the home today there is no furniture or running water, which is not uncommon among many of the preserved plantation homes. One of the most memorable features of this home is an exhibit panel composed of recorded voices of people who once called Hampton Plantation home. While visiting and reading about a historic site provide a chance for the imagination to wander, there is something extremely satisfying about hearing the actual voices from the past.

In this exhibit, you hear William Boykin, born in 1922, whose grandfather worked for Archibald Rutledge, and Sue Collington Alston (circa 1879–1973), who tells a story about the generational difference between her and her great-great-grandchildren that just tugs at your heartstrings. Gabriel Myers, born circa 1865 at the neighboring Peafield Plantation, whose parents worked in the rice fields, gives his heartbreaking testimony of leaving Santee and going to work "chipping boxes on a turpentine farm near McClellanville." His task was 5,000 boxes a week, for which he was paid fifty cents for every thousand completed, illustrating just how hard people worked after slavery for little or no pay.

Hampton Plantation stayed in the family for about 220 years until Archibald Rutledge, a descendant of the Rutledge family as well as South Carolina's first poet laureate, sold the house to the State Parks of South Carolina in 1971. The plantation does not shy away from its complicated past as a witness to some of the darkest hours in our nation's history, but it highlights how some of the first founding families of South Carolina lived over two centuries.

Heyward-Washington House

87 Church St.
Charleston, SC 29403
charlestonmuseum.org

CHARLESTON'S REVOLUTIONARY WAR HOUSE

Nestled between a row of homes in a Charleston neighborhood, directly across from the Isaac Mazyck House, the Heyward-Washington House faces out toward Church Street. Built by Colonel Daniel Heyward circa 1772, the Georgian-style double house is an exquisite survivor of the colonial era.

Born on James Island in 1720, Heyward married Elizabeth Simons and had five sons and one daughter. A Loyalist to the crown, Heyward made quite a name for himself, building a tidal mill, textile factory, and export-import business on the grounds of his 1740 Old House Plantation. With his business acumen, he turned a land grant of 500 acres into more than 16,000 acres.

Thomas Heyward Jr. was the eldest son of the colonel, born in Beaufort County in 1746. With his father's firm belief in education, Thomas was extremely studious. Accepted to Cambridge University to practice law in 1765, by 1770 he was admitted to the bar by the Inns of the Court. Over the course of the next few years, he traveled to other European countries learning about their governments and their countrymen. These observations would assist in his participation in regulatory roles in structuring America, and upon his return to the colonies at the age of twenty-nine, Thomas became a delegate to the Second Continental Congress in early 1776.

Sympathetic to American causes, Thomas voted for his country's independence on July 4, 1776. He later signed the Declaration of Independence on August 2 of the same year, much to his father's dismay. Additionally, he signed the Articles of Confederation in 1778. Serving as an artillery officer with the South Carolina militia and as a patriot leader during the Revolutionary War, Thomas was taken as a prisoner of war when the British captured Charleston in 1780. Exiled to St. Augustine, Florida, he was paroled in 1781 and continued to serve his country as a circuit court judge from 1781 until 1789.

Thomas's first wife Elizabeth Matthews died during childbirth in 1782 but gave him one son by the name of Daniel who lived into adulthood. His second wife, Elizabeth Savage, birthed three children who all survived. Thomas inherited the Church Street house after his father's death in 1777 where the Heywards resided when not at their own plantation called White Hall. Turning his attention to agricultural life, Thomas helped found the South Carolina Agricultural Society in 1785 as he took on the responsibilities of his own plantation as well as his father's.

While the Heywards were away at White Hall, the city of Charleston rented out the Church Street home to President George Washington while he toured the southern states in 1791. Thomas sold the house in 1794, and it changed hands numerous times until becoming H.W. Fusler & Sons Bakery in the 1880s. In 1929, The Charleston Museum purchased the property, converting it into a house museum soon after. The house contains the original laundry, kitchen, and servants' quarters built by gunsmith John Milner in the 1740s; its floor plan, however, is constructed in the familiar Charleston double style with four rooms on each floor and a central passage. Interesting pieces such as portraits of the Heywards and authentic Charleston-made furniture are present, including the rare Holmes-Edwards bookcase. Serving his country in more ways than one, Thomas Heyward Jr. will be remembered as an American patriot, judge, and agriculturalist.

Hobcaw Barony

22 Hobcaw Rd.
Georgetown, SC 29440
hobcawbarony.org

A BOUNTIFUL LAND

Numerous plantations once occupied the area known as Hobcaw Barony. Perched on the edge of the Waccamaw River, this bountiful land was named by the Waccamaw Indians. Colonizers came into contact with the territory when King Charles II issued a land grant to assist in populating the new colony of Carolina. Sir John Carteret claimed the barony as his own in 1718. With the dissolution of the province due to poor management, King Charles reclaimed the land in 1719, and it became a royal colony in 1729. In 1730, Carteret sold the territory to the crown after which it was split and sold to interested parties.

Colonial plantations named Friendfield (1735), Oryzantia (1794), Bellefield (1794), Calais (1796), and Michau (1796) sprang up over the next fifty years as indigo and rice became major exports and fueled the planter economy. The area thrived until the Civil War left it in financial ruins. Realizing the value of the homes that weren't burned by General Sherman, those who could bought what remained, turning them into hunting grounds and vacation homes. Benard Baruch happened to be one of those people. As a native South Carolinian but also a Jewish New Yorker, his complex story had started a generation before with his father, Simon.

Simon Baruch was born in Prussia during the early nineteenth century. He desired to study and practice medicine, but was unable to because of his Jewish faith. With his parents' blessings, he emigrated to Camden, South Carolina, in the 1850s to stay with the Baum family. The Baums gave young Baruch the opportunity to learn English, earn money, and ultimately pay his way through medical school. When the Civil War broke out, Baruch served as an assistant surgeon for the Confederate Army.

Dr. Baruch returned from war and married Isabelle Wolfe, whose family had been present in America since 1690. The Wolfes were slave owners and a part of Charleston's Sephardic congregation founded in the mid-eighteenh century. The Wolfe family plantation was one of the houses burned during Sherman's raid; yet, the Baruchs stayed. By now, however, the entire makeup of the South had been eradicated, and chaos was inevitable. With a newly freed black population, embittered whites, and financial instability among other factors, extreme violence erupted. Sensing that their livelihood was in danger, the Baruchs took their ten-year-old son Benard and moved to New York City in 1881.

Benard Baruch became a Wall Street millionaire by the time he was thirty-five. Along with his wife Anne, Benard bought 16,000 acres in the Hobcaw Barony for less than $60,000 in 1905. The property would court presidents and family friends alike and become a hunting retreat for years to come. When the original house burned down on December 29, 1929, it was rebuilt and opened by the fall of 1931. In 1935, Benard sold 5,000 acres to his oldest daughter Isabel who loved Hobcaw as much as her father, and by 1956 he had sold her the entire property.

Realizing the value of her family's land Belle continued to steward practices to keep Hobcaw enjoyable for those who came to visit. In 1962 Belle was diagnosed with cancer. Over the next two years, she created an easement where future generations would be able to enjoy Hobcaw as much as she and her family had. Today relationships with various state universities as well as government-run institutions along with the Belle W. Baruch Foundation keep Belle's vision for the land her father adored protected.

Hopsewee Plantation

494 Hopsewee Rd.
Georgetown, SC 29440
hopsewee.com

THE BIRTHPLACE OF A SIGNER OF THE DECLARATION OF INDEPENDENCE

A National Historic Landmark, Hopsewee Plantation was built overlooking the Santee River between 1733 and 1740 by Thomas Lynch and his family. Thomas married Elizabeth Allston who lived on a neighboring plantation, and together they had three children: Sabina, born in 1747; Ester born in 1748; and Thomas Jr., born in 1749. When Elizabeth died six years later in 1755, Lynch married Hannah Motte and together they had Elizabeth in 1755. Thomas Jr. would go on to be one of the signers of the Declaration of Independence in 1776.

The Lynches sold Hopsewee in 1762 to Robert Hume, who lived there until his death in 1766. The property remained in the Hume family in one form or another until the last member left in 1914. Decades later, it was sold to the International Paper Company in 1945, which owned it for two years before selling it to Colonel Reading Wilkinson, whose family continued to own the plantation until 1969 when Mrs. Wilkinson, having successfully raised her children and outlived her husband, swapped the property for a residence owned by Jim and Helen Maynard.

The Maynards, along with their two daughters Cassie and Betts, obtained National Historic Landmark status for the plantation and purchased land originally part of the estate, bringing its total acreage to seventy. Through the years, many developers attempted to purchase the riverfront property, but it was on a visit in 2000 that current owner Frank Beattie convinced the Maynards to sell him Hopsewee Plantation knowing it would remain a private residence.

John Mark Verdier House

801 Bay St.
Beaufort, SC 29902
historicbeaufort.org

THE HEART AND SOUL OF THE LOW COUNTRY

Looking out toward the Beaufort River, the John Mark Verdier House, one of Beaufort's iconic residences, is now surrounded by retail shops, restaurants, and art galleries. This part of downtown has grown into a place where tourists flock to enjoy the town's historic charm, breezes from the waterfront, dining, and shopping.

As one of the oldest structures on Bay Street, the circa 1804 Verdier House is a flashback to how waterfront real estate appeared during the early nineteenth century. Beginning as a parcel of land granted by King Charles II in 1663, the area was divided into plots to be sold. The town of Beaufort was founded in 1711, the same year the Carolina colonies separated into north and south regions.

As a historic house museum, and the only historic house open to the public in Beaufort, the Verdier House provides the community with an excellent facility through which to promote a deeper appreciation for the rich history and architecture of Beaufort. In the years immediately preceding the Revolutionary War, John Mark Verdier, the son of a French Huguenot immigrant, began his rise to prominence as both merchant and planter, with his life reflecting the economic cycles that occurred during his lifetime.

Indigo, which produced the sought-after dye, was Beaufort's principal crop. Its cultivation provided many fortunes, including the Verdier's. However, the war impacted his finances, resulting in serving time in a

Charleston debtors' prison. Verdier returned to Beaufort and capitalized on the next wave of prosperity brought by Sea Island cotton, the finest and most expensive cotton grown in the US. The immense wealth of this period is reflected in the many mansions built in the city at the time, including Verdier's.

Verdier was able, through his holdings, to purchase more land, and his wealth grew substantially. Records show him owning 216 slaves as well as acreage in both St. Helena's and St. Luke's Parishes. Unfortunately, the bubble of his success burst rapidly, perhaps an omen for what would befall his fellow merchants and planters thirty-four years after his death in 1827.

Union Commodore Samuel DuPont sailed into Port Royal Sound just five miles away as the Civil War began. As Union troops moved closer, Beaufort's white population dispersed, leaving their finely built mansions to Union occupation. Homes and businesses were not destroyed as they were in Atlanta, Savannah, Charleston, and Columbia, as Beaufort was protected by this Union occupation when General Sherman's troops passed through in 1865. The federal government had seized most of the homes and businesses and many families who had moved away were financially unable to reclaim their properties. The Verdiers were among the few to get their home back. The home remained in the family until the 1930s, when it was condemned due to negligence after a period of commercial use. Bought by the Historic Beaufort Foundation in 1967, the house is a significant part of Beaufort's architectural history.

Architecturally, it mimics Beaufort's Barnwell-Gough House as well as the Tabby Manse House. Its ground floor is constructed with a tabby mixture composed of crushed oyster shells from the shoreline and lime. Its walls and foundation stand strong. Its exterior is graced with Tuscan columns and pedimented porticoes. Inside, the first-floor hall is flanked by a parlor and formal dining room. Upstairs an elongated ballroom and three additional bedrooms are present. Glimpses of original wallpaper and exposed wood add character to the unfurnished second floor.

Tours opened to the public in 1972, and since then the foundation has continued to improve, restore, and preserve one of the last standing pre–Civil War homes of Historic Beaufort. Today, with Beaufort's growth as a tourist destination, the Verdier House is the center of interpretation of the rich architectural heritage that makes the community so attractive to visitors and residents alike.

Joseph Manigault House

350 Meeting St.
Charleston, SC 29403
charlestonmuseum.org

CHARLESTON'S HUGUENOT HOUSE

Built in 1803, the Joseph Manigault House is a beautiful example of the Adam style, popular during the mid- to late nineteenth century. Named for the Adams brothers who emigrated from Scotland, the uniformed neoclassical aesthetic was a favorite of well-to-do middle- and upper-class homes. Features of the style include symmetry and balance as well as the use of bright paint colors such as blues, greens, and yellows.

Patterned as a parallelogram, the shape of the house alone is unique. Not fashioned in the typical single or double Charleston format, the Manigault House displays a hipped slate roof, high ceilings, and two-story piazzas. Additionally, numerous windows, a cantilevered stairwell, and a signed Robert Walker sideboard contribute to this home's allure. Although the external dependencies are no longer standing, sketches from archaeological excavations provide an insight on what life was like for not only the Manigaults but the people who served them.

The Manigaults were French Huguenots who fled from France in the 1600s fearing religious persecution. Settling along the Santee River, the first generation served as indentured servants; then they became merchants, brandy distillers, and property owners. The Manigaults opened a boardinghouse within Charleston, the profits of which allowed the family to purchase land on which to cultivate rice. By the time of Gabriel Edward Manigault (1704–1781), the Manigaults owned 47,000 acres of land and around six

hundred slaves, their worth equaling about thirty million dollars in today's currency. Gabriel left a large inheritance to his heir, grandson Joseph receiving his share at the age of twenty-five.

Joseph was born on October 19, 1763. The son of Peter and Elizabeth Manigault, he was educated in Charleston and London. Upon his return, Joseph married his first wife Maria Henrietta Middleton in 1788. Sadly, she died during childbirth three years into their marriage. By 1800, Joseph married Charlotte Drayton of Drayton Hall. At the height of his wealth, Joseph owned five plantations totaling 22,000 acres and upward of 300 enslaved field hands. His residence also required fifteen to twenty-five house slaves. Although not much is known about the Manigaults' slaves, Charlotte did bring her slave Affy from Drayton Hall from time to time. During the 1830s until his death in 1843, Joseph experienced financial hardships. In 1852 Charlotte sold their home as construction for the Charleston & Savannah Railroad began directly across the street.

By the early twentieth century, the house fell into disrepair and was to be razed by the Charleston Motor Company to become a parking lot. In 1920, Nell McColl Pringle and her husband saved the house from demolition thanks to the encouragement of Susan Pringle Frost. In an effort to cover maintenance costs, the home was turned into a tenement and was sold after the crash of 1929. The Charleston Museum bought the property in 1933 thanks to a donation from Mrs. Henrietta Guerard Hartford.

The Manigault House was not restored to its former glory until the late 1940s, opening to the public in 1949. It is run by a knowledgeable staff that dutifully explain the various artifacts throughout the house, including a porcelain plate imported from China bearing the Manigaults' family crest. The in-depth tours of this house museum provide a phenomenal snapshot of Charleston's revered golden age.

Magnolia Plantation

3550 Ashley River Rd.
Charleston, SC 29414
magnoliaplantation.com

GARDEN OF DREAMS

It's impossible to cover the familial history and architectural details of Magnolia Plantation & Gardens in a synopsis, as not going into depth would be a disservice to its legacy. Perhaps we could focus on the period pieces from the early eighteenth century that decorate the house or more importantly the numerous enslaved people who once worked in the surrounding rice fields. Or we could even talk about how the plantation became a historic landmark in 1985 and was saved by the National Trust for Historic Preservation, which now considers the area one of the most endangered for preservation in the US. However, once again that would take a considerable amount of in-depth discussion.

Instead, let's discuss what a visit to Magnolia Plantation offers. Driving down Ashley River Road, you see a long stretch of live oak trees holding onto each other as if giving one another a warm hug. You'll see a sign for Drayton Hall, but that's not the Drayton plantation you're seeking.

About a mile down, there's another sign, this one for Magnolia Plantation & Gardens. That's the one you want. Pulling in before the grounds open allows you to appreciate sun rays as they pierce the Spanish moss above as gravel crunches underneath. A glance to the left and you see Magnolia's main house across a dewy meadow.

The parking lot is empty except for staff who have arrived early and two handsome peacocks who strut as if they are runway models. For thirty minutes all is quiet until the gravel starts crunching from the drove of cars packed with tourists anxiously waiting to park. The peacefulness of the morning is filled with laughter and excitement. Today license plates from states such as Georgia, North Carolina, and as far away as Florida flood the parking lot.

Families exit their cars and head to the ticket kiosk where a plethora of choices are available. There's the nature train, which takes you around the property; the house tour, which discusses the Drayton family; and the From Slavery to Freedom Tour, which focuses solely on the African-Americans who lived and worked at Magnolia until the early twentieth century. For the adventurous, there's a nature boat that takes those brave enough on a bit of a safari through alligator-infested waters. For those less adventurous, the historic gardens are always available to stroll.

The day starts with an orientation video where interviews with those who know the property best are shared, including the last descendant who lived on-site. Beginning with the house tour, take forty-five minutes to learn about the Draytons' wealth, their descendants, and the priceless furniture located throughout the family home. This tour ends with enough time for you to walk briskly to the trolley for the tour of the slave cabins. A short drive away from the main house stands four slave quarters and a smaller building that was used as a smokehouse to cure meat. It is here we learn about the Leach family who continue to work at Magnolia as gardeners and landscapers and who lived in one of the cabins until 1969. Although the tour is only forty-five minutes, one genuinely gets a sense of how hard multiple generations of a people worked to survive.

A café serves lunch fare, providing visitors rest and a moment to reflect. Afterward, there's still so much to see. Walking through old rice fields and blooming flowers, brings you to the river where the boat tour awaits. About forty-five minutes long, this tour includes information on various flora and fauna as large alligators graze in the tall grass. By now the sun is setting, as is a day filled with numerous activities.

McLeod Plantation Historic Site

325 Country Club Dr.
Charleston, SC 29412
ccprc.com/1447/McLeod-Plantation-Historic-Site

UNVEILING FREEDOM'S STORY

The McLeod Plantation Historic Site sits on James Island in Charleston, tucked among oak trees drooping with Spanish moss; its beauty but a veil covering a meaningful and important story. The story of this Sea Island cotton plantation is not just of its owners, the McLeod family, but of others who occupied the place, too. People such as the Dawson family, whom the McLeods enslaved. And George Smothers, a black US soldier, who helped liberate four million people. In contrast to other plantations open to the public, McLeod Plantation Historic Site centers its stories on African-Americans who made up a majority of its population from 1850 through 1990 and their resilience: a 140-year quest for freedom, equality, and justice.

America's wealthy depended on slavery to drive the country's growth. Throughout the South cash crops cultivated by enslaved labor endowed the planter class with wealth and power. Tobacco grew in Virginia, Maryland, and North Carolina; rice thrived along the South Carolina and Georgia

coast; sugarcane fields dominated southeastern Louisiana. Each region experienced success; however, a plant bearing fluffy, white fibers changed everything.

Referred to as "King Cotton" due to its lucrative returns, this crop made the Cotton Belt that formed from Texas to Virginia. As cotton expanded, so did the exploitation of forced human labor and the removal of native peoples. But the plantations of coastal of South Carolina, Georgia, and northern Florida were unique. McLeod Plantation and others produced a long-fiber species called Sea Island cotton. At certain points, it was more than ten times as valuable as its short-fiber cousin grown elsewhere in the belt.

In 1851 William Wallace McLeod acquired the plantation of nearly 1,700 acres. That year, nearly a decade before South Carolina finally seceded, he advocated for secession, declaring the issue of slavery as the primary reason. In 1859 he led Charleston's efforts to reopen the trans-Atlantic slave trade. On the eve of the American Civil War the nearly one hundred men, women, and children he enslaved produced more Sea Island cotton—described as the finest cotton ever cultivated—than any other plantation on James Island.

In 1862 McLeod enlisted as a forty-two-year-old private in the Confederate war effort. That spring, the US military captured and occupied neighboring Folly Island. In response, the Confederates ordered an evacuation of all civilians on James Island. However, rather than evacuate with the McLeod family, ten enslaved people successfully claimed freedom, navigating enemy Confederate lines and finding sanctuary on Folly Island. One of them, young William Dawson, enlisted in the US Navy as a cabin boy. A year later, following President Lincoln's Emancipation Proclamation, Dawson reenlisted as one of the first black US Marines. For the first time in his life, he earned a wage and legally bore arms to fight for his freedom.

Following James Island's evacuation, the Confederate Army occupied McLeod Plantation. The house was military headquarters, and the grounds held commissaries, ordnance depots, and a regimental hospital. By the winter of 1865, the Confederacy was crumbling. Fearful of General Sherman reaching General Grant in Virginia, Confederate troops fled Charleston and James Island. In March 1865 the Massachusetts 55th Volunteer Infantry, a black regiment, made McLeod Plantation its headquarters. Private George Smothers proudly left his signature on the third floor of the McLeod home. Smothers, born enslaved in Virginia, escaped to Indiana with his family on the Underground Railroad. Responding to Frederick Douglass's 1863 call to arms and for free blacks to enlist, Smothers joined the army to help free his enslaved brothers and sisters.

Smothers was here on that March day in 1865 when fellow combatant William Dawson returned to McLeod Plantation and laid claim to forty acres. Earlier, General Sherman had declared that abandoned plantations along portions of the coast from South Carolina to Florida were to be distributed among freed people, up to forty acres per person. It is not known whether Smothers and Dawson met, but it is likely. In less than three years Dawson went from enslaved man to land

owner. By 1870 Dawson and his family were among the most successful Sea Island cotton growers on James Island, even outproducing what they had cultivated when enslaved by William McLeod ten years earlier.

From 1865 to 1868, McLeod Plantation was the James Island Field Office for the Freedman's Bureau. The bureau was established to assist four million freed slaves transition out of enslavement. However, on James Island, bureau agents were also tasked with convincing those like Dawson to voluntarily release their forty acres to the previous owners and enslavers. On James Island former landowners were quite successful in reobtaining their plantations, aided by a smallpox epidemic that killed thousands of freed people. By 1870 the McLeods again made the plantation their home. So began 125 years of history at McLeod Plantation that illustrates the fits and starts African-Americans experienced in their struggle for freedom, equality, and justice.

Generations of African-Americans, caught in the vicious cycle of poverty, discrimination, and violence of the Jim Crow South, lived at McLeod Plantation in terrible conditions. Despite that, their love, family, and faith helped them persevere. In 1990 the last McLeod left the plantation to the Historic Charleston Foundation. By 2015 Charleston County Parks purchased and opened it to the public. Through award-winning interpretation, Charleston County Parks removes the veil through which so many plantations filter their history.

The historic site is presented for what it really was: a private, for-profit, slave-labor camp whose legacy of racism impacts so many. A visit promises not to be typical of plantation museums, but an honest remembrance and acknowledgment of America's past and a place where healing might begin.

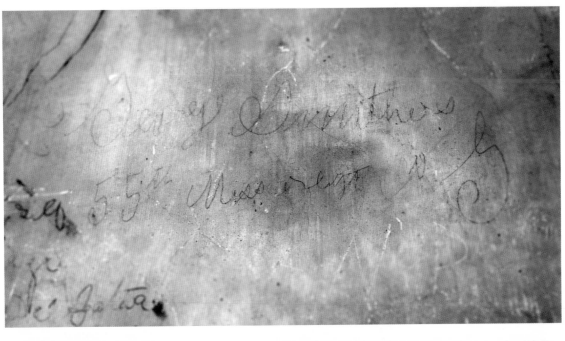

Middleton Place

4300 Ashley River Rd.
Charleston, SC 29414
middletonplace.org

A FOUNDING FAMILY'S HOME

Before the gates open to the public, blonde American Belgian horses from the stables roam free, grazing on Middleton Place's lawn. Behind them, the southern flank of a once three-building property is all that remains. The bucolic scene is a familiar one to early risers who are guests at the Inn at Middleton Place, located less than a mile away from the plantation. Intertwining the eighteenth century with the twenty-first isn't an easy task, yet Middleton Place succeeds in honoring its past, reconciling its present, and preserving its future.

The Middletons' lineage is traceable to the early seventeenth century in England, but it wasn't until two entrepreneurial brothers named Edward (1641–1685) and Arthur (1647–1685) decided to cross the Atlantic Ocean that the Middletons as we know them today came to be. Born to Henry Middleton (1612–1680), the brothers settled in Barbados. Arthur worked as a merchant and Edward dabbled in maritime ventures, trading slaves as well as participating in other economic

endeavors. Edward moved to Charleston first in 1678 and Arthur a year later in 1679. Once settled, the brothers expanded their holdings significantly. The Middletons' network of plantations grew to around twenty-five with their acreage spanning some 63,000 acres and enslaving about 3,500 people.

Edward married Sarah Fowell and had one son, named for his Uncle Arthur who never had any children. Arthur Middleton (1681–1737), Edward's son, had three sons who lived into adulthood: William (1710–1775), Henry (1717–1784), and Thomas (1724–1766). William lived at a palatial plantation called Crowfield, while Thomas moved farther south along the coast settling in the Beaufort area. It was Henry Middleton who acquired the plantation located along the Ashley River through his marriage to Mary Williams (1721–1761). Henry had an astute political career serving as the commissioner of Indian affairs in addition to serving on the First Continental Congress. After Mary's death in 1761, Henry returned to his grandfather's estate The Oaks, relinquishing control of Middleton to his son Arthur (1742–1787) and his wife, Mary Izard (1747–1814).

Henry's son Arthur was a signer of the Declaration of Independence and a prominent figure in the establishment of the young nation. Over the next century, his descendants would experience the Civil War, financial instability, and their ancestral home being burned to the ground in 1865. Understanding the importance of their family history, the Middletons pooled enough money together to start the slow process of rebuilding. The main house and northern flanker were torched as well as looted during the Civil War, and what remained was damaged during the Charleston earthquake in 1886. In 1916 Middleton Place was inherited by J.J. Pringle Smith and his wife Heningham Lyons Ellet Smith, who moved there in 1925 and put extensive work into restoring the grounds and the southern flanker. Recognized by the Garden Club of America in 1941, the Smiths received the coveted Buckley Medal.

While some guests decide to stay at the inn or dine at the Low Country restaurant that pays homage to the famous author, chef, and educator Edna Lewis, others choose to embark on the Beyond the Fields tour, which attempts to highlight those enslaved not just at Middleton Place but throughout the family's entire network of plantations. Taking place in Eliza's House, named after Eliza Leach the last African-American to live at Middleton Place, the tour takes you through the grounds and South Carolina's version of slavery. This attention to detail is significant to note, as though all southern colonies participated in slavery, each had a system that worked better for their specific territory.

Presently operated by the Middleton Place Foundation established in 1974, the site serves as a place to continuously learn and explore.

Nathaniel Russell House

51 Meeting St.
Charleston, SC 29401
historiccharleston.org

FROM ONE SLAVE PORT TO ANOTHER

A Bristol, Rhode Island, native, Nathaniel Russell was born on November 16, 1738. Twenty-seven years later, in 1765, he settled in Charleston, where he became a shipping merchant. Exporting cargo such as cotton, indigo, and rice, he also imported a variety of goods from the West Indies and Great Britain, including humans. Both Bristol and Charleston seaports participated in the trans-Atlantic slave trade, and as a trader, Russell became extremely wealthy.

Russell married Sarah Hopton on June 10, 1788. Sarah was the daughter of William Hopton, a wealthy merchant in the early eighteenth century. The Russells had two children, Alicia born in 1789 and Sarah in 1792. Alicia married one of the most eligible bachelors at the time Arthur Middleton in 1809, while Sarah married Reverend Theodore Dehon in 1813.

Facing Meeting Street, the Nathaniel Russell House sits less than half a mile away from Charleston's seawall, also known as The Battery. Built in 1808 the 9,600-square-foot, Neoclassical structure stands three stories high with two, four-sided bay windows facing south. Its east entrance is recognizable by an entryway of two massive doors made of pine. Walking over a checkered floorcloth, those who were visiting for business sat in an open waiting area next to Nathaniel's office. However, guests of the Russells would continue through another set of double doors and be greeted by a cantilever elliptical spiral staircase.

The first floor hosts a formal dining room with curved doors typical of the Adamesque style, as well as a piece by Charlestonian cabinetmaker Robert Walker that dates circa 1795. Though the central stairwell is off-limits, a set of hidden stairs

once used by the Russells' enslaved servants, is currently available to access the second floor. On the second floor, decorated with twent-four-karat gold, a brightly lit room on the east end of the house was used by Mrs. Russell and her friends for tea. A harp, a pianoforte, and a lyre-guitar, traditional to the period, are found in the drawing room, based on the family's inventory.

Nathaniel Russell died in 1820 and Sarah two years later. Her will left the property in the care of her two daughters and grandchildren. The house remained in the Russell family for almost fifty years until it was purchased by Robert Francis Withers Allston, sixty-seventh governor of South Carolina and his wife, Adele Petigru Allston in 1857.

The Allstons lived in the house for thirteen years before selling it to the Sisters of Charity of Our Lady of Mercy, who held the property for twenty-five years, until 1905. Sold back into private ownership, the house was purchased by the Historic Charleston Foundation in 1955. Eighteen years later, in 1973, the 210-year-old home was designated a National Historic Landmark.

Exiting through the landscaped gardens, visitors may catch a whiff the sweet-smelling star jasmine (Confederate jasmine), a flower that grows well in South Carolina's sweltering heat. As with anything predominately Southern, it beckons you to stay while politely pushing you out the door.

Snee Farm Plantation: Charles Pinckney National Historic Site

1254 Long Point Rd.
Mt Pleasant, SC 29464
nps.gov/chpi/index.htm

HOME TO ONE OF AMERICA'S FOUNDING FATHERS

Spanning three generations, Snee Farm Plantation, also known as the Charles Pinckney National Historic Site, began as a 500-acre land grant given to Richard Butler in 1696. After changing hands a few times, by 1754, the property was owned by Colonel Charles Pinckney and had grown to 715 acres. His son, also Charles Pinckney, born in 1757, is considered one of America's founding fathers. Pinckney had a prominent career in politics serving as the thirty-seventh governor of South Carolina, a US senator, and as the US minister of Spain. As an important piece of America's colonial history, Congress established the plantation as a historic site in 1988. Today the once large plantation is now a twenty-eight-acre property operated by the National Park Service.

While the original house and outbuildings from the Pinckneys' time no longer remain, an 1828 farmhouse and its surrounding structures do. Tours are self-guided, but films such as *Forgotten Founder, Founding Brothers: Sides of Slavery*, and *The Birth of the Constitution* can all be viewed in under an hour. Outdoor activities include a half-mile walking trail to explore the area's agricultural history.

Sandhills Region

South Carolina is a great place to be from.

TIM SCOTT

Composed of small hills and flatland with sandy soil, the Sandhills is where cities such as Camden, Aiken, Lexington, and Columbia, the state's capital, are located. Extremely hot with rapidly flowing rivers, the area was once at sea level millions of years ago until the waters retreated, leaving behind small sand dunes.

Hampton-Preston Mansion

1615 Blanding St.
Columbia, SC 29201
historiccolumbia.org

TWO HUNDRED YEARS OF HISTORY

Part of the Robert Mills Historic District, the Hampton-Preston Mansion & Gardens stands tall as it celebrates its bicentennial anniversary. Walking through its wrought-iron gates, guests encounter four acres of manicured gardens featuring native and exotic plantings, whose lush green contrasts brilliantly with the mansion's yellow ocher paint color, an aesthetic accurate for 1850. With more than 20,000 square feet of trails recently added to the gardens, the former antebellum estate is a unique place to learn about South Carolina's capital city during the nineteenth century.

Erected for Ainsley and Sarah Hall in 1818 by the building firm of Zachariah Phillips and Robert Yates, the mansion is said to have served as a showroom for Ainsley's imported goods business until 1823. The Halls then sold it to Wade Hampton I and his wife Mary Cantey Hampton. Through

private acquisition and bounty land warrants granted by the federal government, Hampton, a veteran of the Revolutionary War and the War of 1812, acquired large tracts in South Carolina, Mississippi, and Louisiana, where he oversaw the planting of rice, cotton, and sugar.

Hampton, credited as the first in Richland County to use a water-powered gin, had sold a cotton crop valued at $90,000 in 1799. As his cotton and sugar exports grew each year, so did the number of people he enslaved. By 1823, the Niles Weekly Register surmised him to be the wealthiest planter in the South, and three years later it noted that he enslaved an estimated 2,000 people across his plantations at any given time. Some of these men, women, and children labored at the Hampton-Preston Mansion, where they cooked, cleaned, and tended the expansive gardens.

Although Wade Hampton I died in 1835, Mary remained at the residence until her death in 1863. Various children and grandchildren lived at the house beginning in the 1840s, and the household grew so large that the mansion underwent a major expansion between 1848 and 1850, doubling its size. Little is known about the lives of those enslaved at the site, with the exception of siblings Maria and William Walker, enslaved by Mary's and Wade's daughter Caroline Preston, and thirty-one enslaved men, women, and children appraised as part of Mary's estate in 1863. Among them was Harrison, the patriarch of a small enslaved family, who more than twenty-five years earlier had been baptized at Columbia's Baptist Church.

Like her parents, Caroline and her husband, John Preston, profited greatly from slavery, eventually selling their portion of Houmas Plantation in Louisiana as well as 550 people enslaved there for $1,000,000 in 1858.

The Hampton-Preston Mansion survived the burning of Columbia on February 17 and 18, 1865, due in part to the presence of Ursuline nuns seeking sanctuary after their convent burned. Financial difficulties forced the Prestons to sell the mansion in 1872, and it served briefly as the home of Franklin J. Moses in 1873, while Moses served as governor of South Carolina. In 1890 the property became the College for Women, which merged in 1915 with Chicora College. Like all educational institutions in South Carolina during the Jim Crow period, both colleges were segregated and admitted only white women. Chicora College departed Columbia in 1930 when it merged with Queen's College in Charlotte, North Carolina.

In 1944 the mansion reopened as the Hampton-Preston Tourist Home. The property rented twenty-five rooms to short-term tourists and long-term boarders until 1966. As part of the Midlands Tricentennial celebration, the mansion reopened to the public as a house museum in 1970, and Historic Columbia took over daily operations in 1972. With a mission to interpret and share the stories of everyone who lived at the site, Historic Columbia's transparency may change the dialogue among visitors for years to come.

Historic Brattonsville:
Colonel William Bratton House and Dr. John Bratton Homestead House

1444 Brattonsville Rd.
McConnells, SC 29726
chmuseums.org/brattonsville

CAROLINA'S FRONTIER

Less than 30 miles from the state line dividing North and South Carolina, a cluster of buildings is all that remains of a once thriving settlement called Brattonsville. In the 1700s, Scotch-Irish pioneers began to settle the western frontier as the New England and Mid-Atlantic colonies became more restrictive. Families traveled along the Great Wagon Road, which extended from Pennsylvania to Georgia, to inhabit the unspoiled southern territories.

The Carolinas split into northern and southern colonies in 1712, yet disputed lands took longer to survey. William Bratton and his wife Martha Robertson, settled on the South Fork of Fishing Creek in York County in 1766. Purchasing 200 acres from Thomas Rainey that same year, Bratton and his wife started their family soon after, having a total of eight children.

The construction date of the Brattons' log cabin is unclear, but the single-pen log structure was standing by 1769. On May 4, 1769, William received a colonial land grant of 200 acres in Tryon County, North Carolina, but sold it in 1771. By 1772, boundary lines for the surveyed land between the two Carolina colonies were finally drawn, including Tryon County. The southern part of the county integrated into South Carolina and became known as The New Acquisition.

As a landowner, Bratton was at the forefront to defend his land when the Revolutionary War broke out in 1775. Appointed as a captain in 1775, he ascended the ranks to colonel by 1779. Battles occurred throughout the Carolina frontier, but on July 12, 1780, it reached the Brattons' door. The Battle of Huck's Defeat holds significance, as a surrender was negotiated by an American army commander, Major General Benjamin Lincoln, and a British army commander, Sir Henry Clinton.

A war tale often untold is about Bratton's slave Watt. A day before the Battle of Huck's Defeat, Martha Bratton tasked Watt with delivering a letter to her husband alerting him that Captain Christian Huck had stationed in the area. Thanks to Watt's bravery in getting the letter delivered, Bratton and the militia returned for a surprise attack before dawn. A plaque erected in Watt's honor sits next to the colonel's cabin.

When Bratton died in 1815, he left the plantation along with 200 acres to Martha and divided his slaves among her and their children.

In his seventy-five years, Colonel William Bratton lived an adventurous life settling the Carolina frontier and fighting for a young country's ideology. His courageous accomplishments will forever be a part of York County's history.

A FAMILY OF DOCTORS

Born to Colonel William and Martha Bratton in York County, South Carolina, on February 21, 1789, Dr. John Simpson Bratton was the youngest of the colonel's sons. He, like his older brother William Jr., studied medicine in Philadelphia. After graduating from Jefferson Medical College, Dr. Bratton returned home to open his practice.

Inheriting most of his parents' estate, Dr. Bratton increased his influence by becoming a cotton planter and merchant. After he married Harriet Rainey from a neighboring plantation in 1814, the couple had fifteen children, fourteen living into adulthood. Previously living in the colonel's log cabin, the Brattons needed a bigger house to accommodate their growing family and showcase their social standing. Construction of their two-story, Federal-style home began in 1823 and took three

years to complete. The original seven rooms consisted of four bedrooms upstairs, with a parlor, study, and breakfast room. Its wings were added after 1826.

Dr. Bratton understood the importance of education and, in 1839, remodeled the log cabin into a school for young women where his daughters could attend. The school opened in 1840 as the Brattonsville Female Seminary. Under the tutelage of Mrs. Catherine Ladd, lessons included skills such as natural science and quill penmanship.

By 1840 the plantation had increased from 200 acres and 12 slaves to 3,540 acres and 112 slaves. The homestead ran as a cotton plantation; however, corn and grains were also grown. Dr. Bratton continued to expand his landholdings throughout York County until his unexpected death in 1843. At the time, he owned 139 slaves and 8,000 acres of land. Probate records show that Dr. Bratton issued large amounts of credit to the community, leaving at least $50,000 of debt against his estate. Harriet recouped some but not all the debt owed to the family. His possessions were divided among his wife and surviving children, inclusive of slaves worth over $40,000.

The Southern slave-based economy and agricultural system collapsed following the end of the Civil War, which irrevocably affected the Brattons' bottom line. When Harriet died in 1874, however, all was not lost. Many of her children had become physicians, businessmen, or married into well-to-do families. The plantation practiced sharecropping until the late nineteenth century, later becoming a tenant farm until the mid–twentieth century.

Local stewards purchased parts of the Brattons' land and surrounding dependencies over the course of the next few decades. The York County Historical Commission was founded in 1963 and managed Colonel Bratton's cabin. The area was designated the Brattonsville Historic District in 1971 and opened to the public in 1976. The historical commission expanded its control over the years to care for the cluster of thirty structures, later renamed Historic Brattonsville.

Today Historic Brattonsville operates as an 800-acre site that provides a snapshot of rural life through the eyes of the Bratton family and their descendants.

Kershaw-Cornwallis House

222 Broad St.
Camden, SC 29020
historiccamden.org

A British-Occupied Home

The home you see today at 222 Broad Street is a replica built in the 1970s. Union troops torched the original structure after the Civil War, although some accounts put the blame on Confederate troops. Cared for by the Historic Camden Foundation, the property includes an outdoor museum with more than 100 acres and other historical structures relevant to Camden such as McCaa's Tavern, built circa 1800, and the eighteenth-century Craven House. Known as Historic Camden today, the foundation started as the Camden District Heritage Foundation in 1966, ten years before Camden's bicentennial in 1976. The museum opened in 1970 and has more than 20,000 visitors each year.

Around the bend and across an open field sits the Kershaw-Cornwallis House. This Georgian-style home boasts double-stacked verandas held up by identical sets of six Doric columns. Twelve nine-paned windows face westward, four on each floor. An elevated brick basement supports two wooden levels perched above. Before walking up the front steps, peek around its left side to see a stone plaque acknowledging that the current house stands precisely where the first structure did in 1777.

The main room contains period furniture sparsely spread along the walls. A portrait of Andrew Jackson, seventh president of the United States, hangs above the mantel. Captured by British troops during the Revolutionary War at thirteen years old,

Jackson was imprisoned at a local Camden jail in 1781. He remains the only president who was a prisoner of war. Another essential artifact hangs on the adjacent wall. The circa-1825 landscape painting depicts the house before it burned down. As one of very few paintings and photographs of the original Kershaw-Cornwallis House, it served as a template for the manor built today.

A print of a Joseph Kershaw, the town's founder and owner of the original house, sits on top of a side table. It is unclear if the picture is of Kershaw Sr. or one of his sons. Kershaw Sr. emigrated from Yorkshire, England, to the Carolina colony in the late 1740s. As a merchant, he established a store in Charlestown, later moving from the coast into South Carolina's interior. His fortune allowed him to build Camden's infrastructure. Kershaw married Sarah Mathis in 1762, and the couple had eight children. Elected to the Commons House of Assembly in 1769 and later the First (1775) and Second (1775–1776) Provincial Congresses, Kershaw had a stellar political career. He continued to serve as part of the General Assemblies throughout the Revolutionary War period (1776–1783), and in 1791 he became Camden's first mayor.

The Battle of Camden took place on August 16, 1780, a few miles from Kershaw's home. British troops captured Kershaw, then a colonel in the state militia, soon after the battle and exiled him to the West Indies. The house became the headquarters to General Charles Cornwallis, First Marquess Cornwallis in June 1780. While he and his military advisors decided their next move, they banished Sarah and her children to live upstairs. Her brother Samuel rescued the family, and they spent the remainder of the war in Burndale, their country plantation home. Almost a year later in 1781, British troops destroyed the city and left Camden, a few months before Cornwallis surrendered in Yorktown, Virginia. Kershaw made it back to his beloved home after the war, where he remained until his death on December 28, 1791.

Kershaw's contribution and commitment to the Patriots' plight define why his home is a cornerstone of American history.

Magnolia Dale

320 Norris St.
Edgefield, SC 29824
historicedgefield.com

TEN GOVERNORS PROUD

South Carolina's history stems back to the 1663 grant by King Charles II of England to the eight Lords Proprietors who had assisted him in returning to the throne. This grant encompassed all of the land from Virginia to Spanish Florida and included the present states of North and South Carolina and Georgia with the grant extending, theoretically, to the Pacific Ocean. Settlement of the Carolina colony began with the establishment of Charles Town in 1670.

Some eighty years later, around the middle of the eighteenth century, settlers began to drift into the area now known as Edgefield County. One of the first families to settle here was the Youngblood family who arrived in 1764. Peter Youngblood purchased a tract of 400 acres on Beaverdam Creek and, with his family, settled the town of Edgefield. Their house was constructed on the site where Magnolia Dale now sits. Other families moved into the neighborhood in the years following. In 1773 the Youngblood family sold 300 acres of their property to a newly arrived Virginian named Arthur Simkins (1742–1826), who would become known as the "Father of Edgefield."

Following the Revolution in 1785, the South Carolina Legislature, in its effort to establish more convenient and effective local government, divided the backcountry of South Carolina into a number of new counties, of which Edgefield was one. The site of the courthouse and jail for the new county was just a short distance from the Youngblood home. The village of Edgefield Courthouse grew up around these public buildings.

Arthur Simkins's daughter, Nancy (1769–1843) married Peter Youngblood's son, George, and had a number of children, including Erasmus J. Youngblood (1800–1887) who inherited the Youngblood house. In 1843, the original house burned and Erasmus Youngblood sold the property to Samuel Brooks of Middlesex, Connecticut, who then built Magnolia Dale. The Brooks family lived in the house until Brooks's death in 1867.

Brooks's daughter sold the property in 1873 to Alfred Junius Norris (1839–1900), a former Confederate captain, prominent lawyer, banker, and businessman. Norris enlisted the aid of a local contractor, Austrian immigrant Captain Michael Anton Markert, who enlarged and improved the house. A number of Markert's architectural features still adorn the house.

Alfred Norris was married to Mary Fox (1839–1935) of Lexington. They had one child, a daughter named Mamie, who was born at Magnolia Dale in 1875. At the tender age of twenty, Mamie married twenty-six-year-old James Hammond "Jim" Tillman (1868–1911), a Georgetown University law graduate from a prominent Edgefield County family. Jim's father, George D. Tillman (1826–1901) was the congressman representing this district of South Carolina. Jim's uncle, Benjamin Ryan Tillman (1847–1918), known as Pitchfork Ben, had been the governor of South Carolina from 1890 to 1894 and was then serving in the US Senate, where he remained until his death in 1918.

Ben Tillman was known for his strong support of the small farmers of South Carolina, whom he believed were being hurt by state and national economic policies. He was also a staunch opponent of black citizens participating in the political process and exercising their Fifteenth Amendment rights. He believed he was improving the lives of the people of South Carolina and led in the establishment of Clemson University for men, Winthrop University for women, and South Carolina State University for black citizens.

Jim Tillman became involved in politics as well. He served as lieutenant governor of South Carolina from 1901 to 1903. Largely as a result of the successful newspaper campaign against him by Narcisco G. Gonzales, editor of *The State* newspaper in Columbia, Tillman lost in his bid to become governor of South Carolina in the 1902 election. Deeply embittered by this, on his last day as lieutenant governor, Tillman walked across the street from the State House, where he knew Gonzales would be walking to his midday dinner, and fatally shot Gonzales at point-blank range. In a trial that garnered nationwide attention, Tillman was acquitted of murder. His political career, however, was at an end. He died less than a decade later of tuberculosis.

Mamie Norris Tillman continued to live at Magnolia Dale with her mother. In 1929 she sold the property to the Kendall Company of Boston, Massachusetts, but continued to live there as a tenant. Mamie became the longtime president of the Edgefield County Historical Society and did much to preserve the county's rich history. In 1959 she succeeded in getting the Kendall Company to give Magnolia Dale to the historical society to serve as its headquarters and house museum. She died at Magnolia Dale in 1962, at the age of eighty-seven.

Throughout the years Magnolia Dale has been used by the historical society to showcase Edgefield's rich and multifaceted history. Open by appointment, the house museum contains a large number of interesting artifacts dating from the nineteenth century, including important portraits of prominent Edgefieldians, the dining room table and chairs of Governor Tillman, the sideboard of Governor McDuffie, and a document box of Governor Francis W. Pickens from when he served as US ambassador to Russia from 1858 to 1860. Magnolia Dale is truly a must-see for visitors to this part of South Carolina.

Mann-Simons Site

1403 Richland St.
Columbia, SC 29201
historiccolumbia.org

AN ENTREPRENEURIAL SPIRIT IN THE FACE OF OPPRESSION

Born enslaved in Charleston, South Carolina, in 1799, Celia Mann arrived in Columbia by the early 1840s and obtained her freedom sometime before 1843. In that year, her husband, Ben Delane, transferred this property to her, making her one of the only free women of color to own land before the Civil War. The family maintained ownership through 1970.

In Columbia, Celia worked as a midwife, likely caring for both black and white families, while raising her own children. Ben, a skilled boatman whose ability to navigate the rivers likely helped him purchase his freedom, used his two boats to transport goods between Columbia and Charleston. Ben eventually returned to Charleston, and when Celia died in 1867, she left this property to her oldest daughter, Agnes Jackson. Jackson, known as Agnes Jackson Simons by her death in 1907, raised her eight children at the current home, which was built sometime between 1872 and 1883.

Today the property also features four frame-only structures, known as ghost structures, which represent a second family home, an outhouse, a store, and a lunch counter that stood on the property during the early twentieth century. Signage throughout the site interprets the history of the family and these structures. The home's interior is now a museum dedicated to the family's achievements in the face of hardship during Jim Crow. It uses fragmentary archival records to highlight the difficulty of uncovering the lives of African-Americans in the South and also relies on artifacts found during a years-long archaeological dig at the site to interpret how the family might have once lived.

One of the most jarring pieces discovered is a bottle of White Life, a skin-lightening cosmetic that may have been sold at the property's lunch counter, owned

by John Lucius Simons. White-owned cosmetic companies pushed the idea that lighter skin was more beautiful in the early twentieth century, although the relationship that African-Americans had with these products was more complicated, with some embracing the ability to pass as white and others celebrating their natural beauty.

A pair of large-format photographs featuring Charles Hall Simons and his wife, Amanda Green Simons, hangs in the southeast room. Like his grandmother Celia Mann, who helped found Calvary Baptist Church at this site in 1865, Charles was a man of faith and community, serving as deacon in the church and as a Freemason. Amanda, a dressmaker, was a well-respected woman in the community until her death in 1960.

The last room of the house focuses on how archival sources reveal the extent of segregation leading up to the Civil Rights Movement. Flip through a 1941 Columbia City Directory and find Amanda Simons, listed at this home in a separate "colored" section, and watch television outtakes discussing the opposing, historic views of urban renewal and desegregation in higher education. Threatened by urban renewal in 1970, activists challenged city officials and won the fight to save this historic site from demolition. The property opened to the public in 1978 as a museum.

Since then, input from the Simons family, extensive research, and restoration have contributed to this home's story. As one of the oldest known black-owned sites in the state's capital city, the Mann-Simons Site is an important part of South Carolina's history. The museum within, operated by Historic Columbia, showcases the often-underutilized perspective of an entrepreneurial African-American family thriving during a period of oppression.

Oakley Park Plantation

300 Columbia Rd.
Edgefield, SC 29824
south-carolina-plantations.com

PRESERVATION OF THE SOUTH

Owned and operated by the United Daughters of the Confederacy since 1948, Oakley Park Plantation currently serves as a Confederate museum in Edgefield, South Carolina. A little more than an hour away from the state capital, this nineteenth-century mansion and grounds remind visitors of a once-thriving agricultural livelihood from a bygone era.

Virginia native Daniel Bird moved to South Carolina after the Revolutionary War, acquiring land throughout Edgefield County. In 1784, he purchased 250 acres along Logg Creek and another 270 acres by 1785. Bird owned around forty slaves in 1808, valued at about $10,000. Bird and wife Susannah had four children, and Daniel Jr. followed in his father's footsteps, becoming a wealthy cotton planter. At the age of twenty-two, he married Sarah Wells Oliver in 1806, the same year his father died. When Sarah died a mere six years later, Daniel Jr. waited two years while serving as a captain in the War of 1812 before he married Lucinda Brooks in 1814. Together they had five children: Louisa Ann, Thomas Butler, Caroline, Mary S., and Cornelia Lucia. Fourteen years later, Lucinda died as well, leaving Captain Bird once again a widow.

Less than a year later, in 1827, Captain Bird married again, this time he chose Lucinda's sister, Behetheland Brooks who had previously been married to Jesse Simkins. A year into their union, Captain Bird purchased 174 acres along Shaws Creek in 1828. Between 1828 and 1835, Behetheland bore four children to continue the Bird lineage. Sarah Oliver in 1831, Richard as well as Pickens Brooks in 1833, and William Capers in 1835. With at least nine children at home, Captain Bird decided to build a stately mansion to showcase his wealth, as well as to accommodate his growing brood.

Tragically, Daniel's twenty-two-year-old son Thomas was accidentally shot and killed in a duel between the captain and another man by the name of Colonel Louis T. Wigfall at the Edgefield County Courthouse. Local folklore says Captain Bird was heartbroken over the loss and sold his home to Colonel Marshall Frazier in 1840 before gathering his wife and the rest of his children and settling in Monticello, Florida. He died in 1867.

Agriculturally invested in Edgefield County, Colonel Frazier planted cotton but also sold goods such as bacon, flour, potatoes, and cheese. He served as a delegate for the annual Southern Commercial Convention (SCC), which conferred about how to economically further develop the South.

When Frazier died in 1870, the mansion was once again on the market.

One of the most notable owners of Oakley Park was Confederate Brigadier General Martin Witherspoon Gary. Born in Cokesbury, South Carolina, in 1831, Gary attended Harvard University, graduating in 1854. After passing the bar, he moved to Edgefield and began practicing law. Elected to South Carolina's House of Representatives in 1860, Gary supported the idea of secession. His fiery oratory skills, as well as appearance, led to his nickname the Bald Eagle of Edgefield.

Gary joined the Confederate cavalry under the command of Lieutenant

General Wade Hampton III as an infantry captain. Composed of soon-to-be generals Stephen Dill Lee, J. Johnston Pettigrew, and Matthew C. Butler, Hampton's Legion fought in the First Battle of Manassas. General Gary never surrendered when the war ended in 1865. He escorted President of the Confederate States Jefferson Davis as far as South Carolina, where Gary retired from the Confederate Army at his mother's home in Cokesbury.

General Gary resumed his law practice and later became the leader of South Carolina's division of the Red Shirts, a militia organization that supported the reinstitution of Southern Democrats into political power during the Reconstruction era. Gary served as a representative from Edgefield in the state senate for two terms and was instrumental in Wade Hampton III winning the gubernatorial election of 1876. General Gary died on April 9, 1881, but Oakley Park remained in the his family, as his nephew John Gary Evans came to live with his uncle after the death of his father Nathan George Evans in 1868. At the time of General Gary's death, Evans was seventeen years old. He would go on to live a life of public service, as South Carolina governor from 1894 until 1897, serving in the Spanish-American War, as a delegate to the Democratic National Conventions in various years, and in the South Carolina House of Representatives in 1922.

Although Evans lived in Spartanburg for most of his adult life, in 1941 he bestowed Oakley Park to the town of Edgefield and died a year later in 1942. His final resting place is Willowbrook Cemetery, also known as the Edgefield Village Cemetery, alongside his wife Emily Mansfield Plume Evans of Waterbury, Connecticut.

Ownership of Oakley Park has since been conveyed to the United Daughters of the Confederacy, and many pieces of memorabilia have been donated to the museum, including Confederate currency, flags, and medals. Additionally, there are several pieces of furniture that are original to the house, including a nineteenth-century couch located in the front parlor and General Martin W. Gary's desk. Other heirlooms to look for are the Victorian hair art from members of the Gary family, a quilt crafted by Governor Evans's mother Victoria, and a hat tub.

As with most historic homes, restoration projects take place in waves. Repairs and improvements continue to be made. Well into the twenty-first century, Oakley Park remains a significant memorial to South Carolina's Confederate history.

Redcliffe Plantation State Historic Site

181 Redcliffe Rd.
Beech Island, SC 29862
southcarolinaparks.com/redcliffe

COTTON IS KING

Two miles east of Beech Island, South Carolina, a red clay dirt road leads to a bluff where Redcliffe Plantation is majestically situated. This beautiful country estate was home to four generations of the Hammond family as well as numerous African-American families such as the Henley, Wigfall, and DeWalt families who, among others, lived at the site as enslaved laborers or later as paid employees between 1855 and 1875.

Growing up working class, James Henry Hammond married into the prominent Fitzsimons family, taking their seventeen-year-old daughter Catherine as his wife in 1831. Hammond lived an active life, graduating from South Carolina College in 1825 and going on to practice law for three years in Columbia, South Carolina. Hammond also fancied politics, serving in the US House of Representatives in 1835, as the governor of South Carolina from 1842 to 1844, and as US senator from 1857 until 1860. He infamously coined the phrase "Cotton is king" while giving an impassioned Senate speech on March 4, 1858.

The Hammonds began construction of their Redcliffe Plantation in 1857. Built by Augusta contractor William Goodrich for $20,000, the two-story house was completed in 1859. The 400-acre country estate served as Mr. Hammond's central place of operations for this and his other plantations. Redcliffe's landscape once flowered with apple and peach orchards, as well as other fruit and vegetable crops, and operated as a place of analysis for Hammond. The success of small plots grown at the estate were then practiced on other plantations to cultivate in larger quantities. Owning twenty-two miles of working farms, Hammond enslaved more than 300 people. One farm, called Silverbluff located in Barnwell County, was 7,000 acres and had at least 200 enslaved people who worked its fields harvesting cotton and corn.

Politically conservative, Hammond believed slavery was not a sin but a moral right from God. This belief led to an indifferent treatment of his slaves, which in turn caused a high mortality rate among them. Because of the lengthiness of the Hammonds living on the property, primary documentation spanning over 100 years provides insight into some of the slave families who lived at Redcliffe.

The Henleys were one of those families. Hammond bought Anthony Henley in 1834 and his wife Lucy during the mid-1840s. Lucy worked as a house slave, while Anthony worked in the fields. Two of their children, Victoria and Emma, were two of the first black students to attend the Beech Island Primary school in 1869. Members of the Henley family continued to live at Redcliffe until 1992, 135 years from the time Anthony and Lucy first arrived. A family cemetery is less than a mile away from the house is where many of their ancestors are laid to rest. Voted by the South Carolina African-American Heritage Commission as one of the "Top Ten Sites to Visit in South Carolina," Redcliffe recognizes the Henleys' as well as other African-American families' contribution to this historic home.

According to the 1860 census, Hammond died in 1864 leaving behind $30,000 in real estate and a personal estate worth $40,000. His heirs sold off pieces of the massive estate over the course of the nineteenth and twentieth centuries. Hammond's great-grandson John Shaw Billings, an editor of *Time*, *Life*, and *Fortune* magazines, donated Redcliffe and its grounds to the state in 1973. Today 369 acres surround Redcliffe with a century-old magnolia lane planted in 1860. Rocking chairs grace a semi-wraparound porch that looks out over the horizon. The house museum holds more than 4,000 artifacts, while the Visitors Center Exhibit has literature and photographs that tell generational stories of the black and white families who once called Redcliffe home.

Robert Mills House

1616 Blanding St.
Columbia, SC 29201
historiccolumbia.org

BUILT BY AMERICA'S FIRST FEDERAL ARCHITECT

Originally built for English merchant Ainsley Hall, the Robert Mills House & Gardens are stunning. Born in 1783, Hall emigrated from England to Columbia, South Carolina, around the turn of the nineteenth century and ran a general store on Main Street and worked as a cotton broker. Southern planters relied on brokers to sell their crop at premium prices for an appreciable return on investment. Their dependency on brokers made the position a profitable one.

Hall married Sarah Cooke Goodwyn, whose family owned several plantations in lower Richland County. The marriage increased his wealth and social standing. The Halls' first home, which was built in 1818, stood across the street; they sold it to Wade Hampton I in 1823.

The Halls commissioned Charlestonian Robert Mills to design this home for them. Mills became an architect and engineer for the state's Board of Public Works in 1820. As one of the first American-trained architects, Mills studied under the tutelage of British architect Benjamin Henry Latrobe and Irish architect James Hoban. Latrobe and Hoban's names may sound familiar, as they assisted with the White House's current design. Mills later designed the Washington Monument.

Unfortunately, Hall died in August of 1823 without updating his will to include the new home, leaving Sarah to fight her brother-in-law for its possession in court over the next several years. Construction took almost six years, finishing in 1829. Sarah sold the three-story brick house to a Presbyterian seminary less than a year later. The property would

later serve as a campus for the Columbia Bible College. In 1960, due to negligence, city officials threatened to demolish the property. Local citizens took matters into their own hands, forming Historic Columbia in 1961. Following years of extensive rehabilitation, the organization opened this National Historic Landmark to the public in 1967 as a house museum.

The Robert Mills House is a lovely example of Classic Revival architecture. Its tetra style portico of four Ionic columns evoke similarities to ancient Greek temples. A fanlight window sits above the front door, allowing fractured light to enter its foyer. Inside, a curved entryway showcases an architectural feat for the time. The east parlor's golden tapestries complement teal paint and ruby-colored settee furniture, while the adjacent west parlor holds an antique harp awaiting nimble fingers to grace its strings.

Upstairs traditional museum galleries feature nineteenth-century artifacts, particularly examples from Historic Columbia's impressive silver and ceramics collections. Descending into the elevated basement, one can view a storage room, kitchen, and private eating quarters. The ornamental garden surrounding the mansion is based on formal English design but executed with selections of plants native to eastern North America. Heirloom vegetables sourced from local midlands communities including old-timey Dutch Fork pumpkin, Kibler okra, and white rice peas, and are grown in vegetable beds located behind each of the home's supporting flanker buildings. Historic Columbia has become both an advocate and resource in Columbia and regionally for heirloom and heritage foods of South Carolina. Their determination and dedication to this area's history prevented this architectural gem from being demolished.

Piedmont Region

Mountains are the beginning and the end of all-natural scenery.

JOHN RUSKIN

Formed from the French words *pied*, which means "foot," and *mont*, which means "mountain," the name roughly translates to "foot of the mountains". The region runs from Alabama north through Maine along the Appalachian Mountains. The Blue Ridge Mountains, howerver, are a province of this mountain range, mostly found in the South. Two of the major cities of this region are Greenville and Spartanburg.

Ashtabula

2725 Old Greenville Hwy.
Central, SC 29630
pendletonhistoricfoundation.org

FROM GENERATION TO GENERATION

The house on Ashtabula Plantation was built between 1825 and 1828 by Lewis Ladson Gibbes. After he died at the age of fifty-seven in 1828, his middle son Charles took over operations because Gibbes's eldest son, Lewis Reeve Gibbes moved to Charleston to study medicine. However, in the mid–1830s Charles moved to California to study civil engineering, drafting some of the first maps of the area's gold mines. This left Ashtabula to John Gibbes, the youngest of the three brothers, but he only cared for it briefly and the house went up for sale in 1837.

Ozey Robert Broyles, a scientific agriculturalist, purchased the house and he and his family lived there for fourteen years before they sold it and moved to Anderson County. In 1851 James T. Latta purchased Ashtabula from Broyles and managed the property until 1861, at which time it was purchased by Robert Adger whose brother owned Woodburn Plantation at the time. Adger then gave Ashtabula to his daughter Clarissa Walton and her husband, Orsamus Allen Bowen, as part of her inheritance.

Bowen raised cattle on the plantation's land, providing a considerable amount of beef to the Confederate Army. However, after continuous raids by detachments of the Union calvary, the Bowens decided to move to Charleston. Rodger Adger took over operations again, this time giving the plantation to his second daughter, Sarah Elizabeth, and her husband William Dalton Warren. Making an agreement with former slaves who later became tenant farmers, Warren operated Ashtabula as a plantation until 1880.

In 1880, Francis J. Pelzer purchased and used the home as a weekend residence while he ran textile mills in the neighboring town of Pelzer, his namesake. However, he too, decided to move back to Charleston, and in 1889 he sold the property to John Linley, a real estate developer who used it to cultivate corn and cotton while he lived in his other home in North Anderson. For thirty-one years Linley sustained operations until he sold the house in 1920 to Pendleton native Fred W. Symmes, who was the last private owner of Ashtabula Plantation. His family sold it to the Mead Corporation in 1957, which in turn gave the house and ten acres of land to the Pendleton Historic Foundation for restoration in 1961.

Open on Sunday, the two-story house is surrounded by a 1790 tavern, the oldest brick building in Anderson County, as well as a schoolhouse and kitchen.

Fort Hill

102 Fort Hill St.
Clemson, SC 29634
clemson.edu/about/history/properties/fort-hill

A HOUSE ON THE HILL

Once part of a 1,100-acre plantation, Fort Hill now sits on a five-acre plot amidst Clemson University, surrounded by shrubs and towering trees. Beneath the Carolina sun, its green shutters complement its white wainscoting and heart of pine front door. As part of the Calhoun family, Fort Hill's story began in 1784.

Initially, the state of South Carolina granted 600 acres to Robert Tate who then sold the property to John Ewing Colhoun in the late eighteenth century. Colhoun subsequently deeded the land to Reverend James and Elizabeth McElhenney in 1802. The McElhenneys built a modest four-room house and named it Clergy Hall Plantation. Upon the reverend's death, the estate went back to John Ewing Colhoun's widow, Floride. When her daughter, also named Floride, married John Caldwell Calhoun on January 8, 1811, Calhoun rented Clergy Hall from his mother-in-law until her death in 1836. That same year, the property became his. He had already changed the name to Fort Hill, after Revolutionary War Fort Rutledge. Acquiring adjacent land plots around Fort Hill, Calhoun grew the 600-acre plantation to over 1,000 acres.

Born in Abbeville, South Carolina, in 1782, Calhoun graduated from Yale College in 1804, studied law at the Tapping Reeve's Law School, and was admitted to the bar in 1807. Elected to the South Carolina Legislature in 1808, Calhoun began his revered political ascent. Winning a seat within the US House of Representatives in 1810, he became a part of the War Hawks, who wanted to rage war against Great Britain, ending its imperialistic control. Serving in the House of Representatives until 1817, Calhoun became secretary of war to President James Monroe for eight years until 1825.

Calhoun ran in the 1824 presidential election, but withdrew due to the overwhelming support for his running mates. Shifting his efforts to the vice presidency, he won unopposed and served for two consecutive terms under President John Quincy Adams (1825–1829) and President Andrew Jackson (1829–1832). Calhoun stayed in Washington, D.C. after his vice presidency, continuing as a US senator from 1832 until 1843, secretary of state to President John Tyler from 1844 to 1845, and again as a US senator from 1845 until 1850.

Prior to relocating to the Pendleton District of South Carolina, the Calhouns had an active Washington social life. As second lady of the United States, Floride aided in social protocol following the

death of First Lady Rachel Jackson. Following the Petticoat War with then Secretary of War John Henry Eaton's wife Peggy O'Neal Timberlake Eaton, however, Mrs. Calhoun preferred the quieter life in South Carolina. While her husband was away in Washington, D.C., she managed Fort Hill's plantation affairs, expanding the four-room structure to a fourteen-room mansion by enslaved labor. The Calhoun family included ten children, although only seven lived into adulthood. The family undoubtedly needed more space; however, under her supervision, the construction commenced without an architect, which led to rooms of various lengths and sizes. Floride did add both English and French wallpapers fashionable in the Victorian era. The Fort Hill plantation at that time included between seventy and eighty slaves. While most of them tended the fields, there were skilled tradesmen and women among them, including blacksmiths, carpenters, millers, seamstresses, gardeners, and cooks.

Upon Mr. Calhoun's death in 1850, Floride initiated a bill of sale of Fort Hill to her eldest son Andrew Pickens Calhoun. When Andrew died in 1865, the debt was not paid,

so Floride foreclosed on her daughter-in-law Margaret and reclaimed ownership of the house along with 1,341 acres. Upon her death in 1866, her will left a portion of the estate to the Calhouns'

only surviving child Anna Maria, who, in turn, willed her part of the estate to her husband Thomas Green Clemson upon her death in 1875. Clemson, a Philadelphian by birth, had studied both at Norwich University and later at the Sorbonne. His formal degree was of assayer of mines from the French Royal Mint. He would later serve as chargé de affaires to Belgium at the court of Leopold I and as the first acting US secretary of agriculture. A Renaissance man and philanthropist, Clemson's long career in sciences, art, agriculture, education, and public service led to his bequest.

At his death in 1888, he willed 814 acres and $80,000 to the state of South Carolina. The stipulations of his gift were that an agricultural and scientific college be built and that the Calhouns' home be preserved. A year later, in 1889, the state accepted his bequest and began erecting, initially, Clemson Agricultural College, later Clemson University in his honor.

Operated by Clemson University, Fort Hill is today maintained as a historic house museum and National Historic Landmark complex interpreting the lives of the Calhoun and Clemson family and the enslaved African-Americans who toiled on the plantation.

Hanover House

530 Garden Trail
Clemson, SC 29634
clemson.edu/about/history/properties/hanover

A GALLIC-INFLUENCED GEM

Clemson University has a treasure trove of historic properties on its campus from Fort Hill, home of Vice President John C. Calhoun and Ambassador Thomas G. Clemson, to the Hopewell Plantation, family home of General Andrew Pickens. It seems right that Hanover House also has a place on its manicured grounds. Home to French Huguenot rice planter Paul de St. Julien, this eighteenth-century house was named in honor of King George I, also referred to as the elector of Hanover. The two-story structure is an archetype of Gallic architecture.

Paul's grandparents Pierre de St. Julien Sr. and Jeanne LeFibure, along with their friend Rene Ravenel, fled from religious persecution in France, settling in South Carolina in 1686. Born in the late seventeenth century, Paul married Mary Amy Ravenel, and they had two surviving children, Mary and Elizabeth. Paul died in 1741, leaving his young daughters all of his property, including

forty-five enslaved African-Americans. His will specified that his 1,000-acre plantation known as Hanover was to be inherited by Mary. Interestingly, South Carolina was one of the few colonies where women were allowed to own property. Mary took ownership of Hanover House for almost a decade before marrying Henry Ravenel, her first cousin, in 1750. Together they had a total of sixteen children. Mary died six years before Henry in 1779, he passed sometime before July 5, 1785. Family lore claims that four of their sons fought in the American Revolution in the services of Brigadier General Francis Marion, the pesky militia officer known as the Swamp Fox.

Mary and Henry's son Stephen Ravenel (1771–1818) inherited the Hanover property, and it remained in his possession until 1817, at which time he passed Hanover to his brother Daniel James Ravenel IV (1789–1873), who served as the secretary of state in 1810. About two decades later, Daniel willed the home to his grandnephew Henry LeNoble Stevens (1827–1862), who served during the Civil War and died from a gunshot wound at the Second Battle of Manassas, also known as the Second Battle of Bull Run. The property remained within the Ravenel family until it was sold in 1904 to a hunting association.

Abandoned by tenant farmers in the late 1930s, destruction threatened Hanover House. To accommodate growth in the area, the South Carolina Public Service Authority proposed to build the Pinopolis Dam combining the Cooper and Santee Rivers and creating the man-made Lake

Moultrie. In 1938 the US Department of Interior's associate architect Thomas T. Waterman deemed Hanover House of vital architectural importance; it was already seventy years older than any other house in the area of inundation. Because of this, the Historic American Buildings Survey (HABS) put a plan in motion to have the home relocated to another site. Disassembled piece by piece, Hanover House moved 250 miles from the Charleston area to Clemson College, two hundred years after its original owner's death.

Eventually, the United States entered World War II after the bombing of Pearl Harbor on December 7, 1941. The war led to a two-year halt on the home's reassembly; the reconstruction was completed on November 1, 1945. By 1962, Hanover House had opened to the public thanks to the hard work of the National Society of the Colonial Dames of America (NSCDA), especially the members of the Spartanburg Committee. Rare to Southern architecture, the design of this house is typically seen in France. Paul de St. Julien had intentions for a brick house; however, since the three brick kiln loads had not completed the two chimneys and basement, he decided to use the local lumber for the first and second floors. Hanover's outside siding is a reverse shiplap, which prevented rainwater from entering the home, preserving its current condition. The original basement walls were eight feet high and two feet deep, but of course, the basement remains underneath Lake Moultrie.

Inside the drawing room is an original chair owned by the family as well as a pianoforte made by Joseph Kirkman II that still holds a tune. In the dining room a portrait of Suzanne Ravenel sits above the mantel. The painting is based on another by Henrietta Johnson, copied by Charleston artist Alicia Rhett as a companion to her painting of Rene Ravenel in the parlor. Another family portrait, this one of Mary Ravenel Broughton, daughter of Daniel Ravenel II and Charlotte Mazyck of nearby Wontoot Plantation also hangs in the home. Peek inside the fireplaces and you can see the contrasting brick colors from the various kiln loads used by Paul de St. Julien, while the master bedroom exhibits gorgeous unpainted black cypress walls in their authentic state.

Clemson University, home to the only architecture school in South Carolina, preserved Hanover House as a monument of Colonial architecture for future generations. A destination garden of plants studied by early naturalists William Bartram, Andre Micaud, and Mark Catesby provides a welcoming educational experience.

Hopewell Plantation

101 Fort Hill St.
Clemson, SC 29634
clemson.edu/about/history/properties/hopewell

REVOLUTIONARY FAMILY HOME OF
GENERAL ANDREW PICKENS

Today Hopewell Plantation sits quietly on the shoreline of Lake Hartwell, yet, more than two hundred years ago, the up–country farm was a bustling center of trade. The land had been home to the Cherokee Indians prior to the American Revolution. The village of Esseneca was located near the confluence of the Keowee and the Twelve Mile River, which formed the Seneca River. Native Americans settled at the hair-pin turn, slowed the current, and provided a ford of the stream that allowed for portions of the village on both sides of the river. William Bartram visited Esseneca twice during his travels, describing the Cherokee town and residents.

It was on this land that negotiations between the Native Americans and the new American govern-ment would take place. Born on September 13, 1739, Andrew Pickens of Paxtang, Pennsylvania, would eventually find himself a big player in these negotiations.

When he was a young teenager, his family traveled along the Great Wagon Road settling along Wax-haw Creek in 1752. By 1765, Pickens had met young Rebecca Floride Calhoun and the two had married and moved to Abbeville, South Carolina. Beginning their family two years later, the Pickens went on to have twelve children who would continue the family's legacy of service.

In 1775 Pickens reported for military duty during the Snow Campaign to Continental commander Brigadier General Andrew Williamson. He went on to participate in the Battle of Seneca Town (1776), in which his comrade, Francis Salvador, would be remembered as the first Jewish-American patriot to die in the Revolution. Pickens would later garrison his men at the wooden stockade Fort Rutledge as a frontier outpost.

With the surrender of the British in 1783, the now-General Pickens returned home to his family. Due to his valiant efforts, he was able to obtain a sizable land grant from the state of South Carolina in 1784. He purchased 573 acres along the Seneca River on May 21, 1784, and an additional 560 acres on March 25, 1785. Shortly after, the construction of his first residence on the Hopewell Plantation commenced.

Elected to public office, Pickens served in the South Carolina House of Representatives and in the Third US Congress. He also acted as a commissioner of Indian Affairs, in which capacity he would meet with representatives of the Southern Tribes, along with Benjamin Hawkins, Joseph Martin, and Lachlan MacIntosh on behalf of the new United States and sign the Hopewell Treaties with the Cherokee in 1785 and with the Choctaw and Chickasaw in 1786. The acceptance of each agreement occurred under a huge oak tree on the Hopewell Plantation, later referred to as the Treaty Oak, which stood into the early twentieth century. Native-American delegations included Chief Corn Tassel, the Beloved Woman of the Cherokee Nancy Ward, Chief Piomingo of the Chickasaw nation, and Chief Yockonahoma of the Choctaw nation. Pickens was a popular choice to lead the negotiations, as he had been given the name Skyagunsta or Wizard Owl by the Cherokee during the Revolution.

Pickens was also a slave owner, and he developed a special friendship with his manservant Richard Pickens. Richard fought in the Battle of Cowpens in 1781 with Pickens. Upon his death, General Pickens requested the freedom of Richard, his wife Fillis, as well as six other slaves by the names of Jame, Seala, Bob, Clarase, Sambo, and July. Additionally, the eight slaves were to receive land, livestock, and the tools needed to survive. Sadly, it is unknown if this occurred. Hopewell's slave history is a work in progress, but a nearby antebellum cemetery at Cherry Farm has the graves of African-Americans from the antebellum period to the early twentieth century.

Hopewell Plantation's history and structures are being researched, and a master plan is underway to restore the house and interpret the evolution of the site in the antebellum era. Locations of the outbuildings have already been found utilizing ground-penetrating radar. As written on his epitaph at the nearby Old Stone Church, where Andrew Pickens served as a Presbyterian elder, "He was a Christian, a Patriot & Soldier: His Character & actions are incorporated with the history of his Country." General Andrew Pickens's bravery and political astuteness undoubtedly contributed to America's independence.

Rose Hill

2677 Sardis Rd.
Union, SC 29379
southcarolinaparks.com/rose-hill

THE SECESSION GOVERNOR

Within Sumter National Forest, century-old magnolias shade the pale two-story house of Rose Hill. Before its restoration, the Georgian-style home belonged to Governor Willam Henry Gist. Born August 22, 1807, in Charleston, South Carolina, Gist was the illegitimate son of Francis Fincher Gist and Mary Boyden. Francis died in 1819, leaving a vast amount of land for his son in upper Union County. Increasing his land, Gist acquired much of his wealth as a slaveholder and cotton planter. At the height of Rose Hill's production, Gist owned 178 slaves.

After attending South Carolina College, now known as the University of South Carolina, Gist married his first wife Louisa Bowen in 1828. Though she died during childbirth, their daughter survived. William remarried Mary Elizabeth Rice in 1832. By the age of thirty-three, Gist was

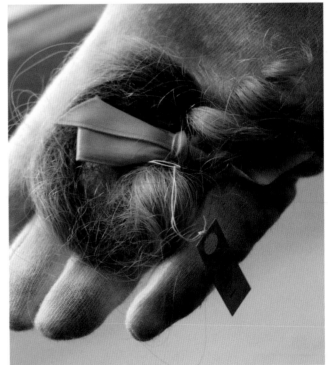

drawn to a career in politics and served two consecutive terms in the South Carolina House of Representatives from 1840.

As tensions over slavery cast the nation into turmoil, Gist defended his belief in slavery as well as his support of secession from the federal government. To the southern states' dismay, Abraham Lincoln won the 1860 presidency. For Democrats, it was the catalyst needed to move forward with secession. Gist, along with other leaders, signed the Ordinance of Secession on December 20, 1860, and South Carolina became the first slave state to secede from the Union. Gist's gubernatorial term ended three days before secession, but his loyalty to the Southern cause did not waver. After the war ended, Gist returned to Rose Hill, where he died in 1874.

The Gist family rented the land and house to tenant farmers until the early 1930s. Around the same time, the US Forest Service began to buy abandoned plantations in Union County. They purchased Rose Hill in 1938. In partnership with the Civilian Conservation Corps (CCC), they planted trees in the area. Today those trees form Sumter National Forest.

In 1942 the Daughters of the American Revolution (DAR) began to look for a sponsor and found one in Clyde T. Franks, an antiques collector and representative of the Federal Land Bank. That same year he bought Rose Hill and its surrounding forty-four acres, immediately undertaking the restoration process. He replaced the wooden porch with brick, repaired the railings with detailed iron, and added period furniture to each room.

In 1960, Franks sold Rose Hill to the South Carolina State Park Service. Today, it is one of the few remaining antebellum homes in South Carolina's upper region.

Seay House

106 Darby Rd.
Spartanburg, SC 29306
spartanburghistory.org/seay-house

SPARTANBURG'S OLDEST HOUSE

Built circa 1831, Seay House is considered Spartanburg's oldest house within its city limits. Named after Kinsman Seay, the one-room log cabin housed his wife Elizabeth and their eight children. The 100 acres around their home were used to plant vegetables and raise livestock, becoming a well-run working farm. Seay inherited the farm from his father Jamie Seay, who fought in the Revolutionary War and moved to the area to start a new life of his own. Living until he was 100 years old, Seay instilled hard work and survival in his son.

Out of Kinsman and Elizabeth's eight children, five moved away to start their own family farms; however, three of his daughters, Ruthy, Patsy, and Sarah, stayed with their parents and assisted in the ever-present farmwork. When Seay passed away in 1887, he left the farm to his three unmarried daughters. While it was rare for women to own property at this time, the Seay sisters continued to make a living for themselves as well as becoming brokers, another anomaly, by loaning amounts of money ranging from $35 to $350 with interest. It is thought that Ruthy, Patsy, and Sarah inherited money from their father and used it to expand the cabin from a single room to the four-room house you see today. The sisters passed away in the early twentieth century, leaving their home to nephew A.J. Dorman.

Operated by the Spartanburg County Historical Association and open the third Saturday of each month, the house holds artifacts such as a spinning wheel and older loom donated by Seay descendants, many of whom still live in the area. In October those descendants come together to have an informal reunion at Seay House for further talks about family genealogical research. At almost two hundred years old, the Seay House has neither been forgotten nor forsaken as the story of the Seay family, particularly the trio of sisters, lives on year after year.

Walnut Grove Plantation

1200 Otts Shoals Rd.
Roebuck, SC 29376
spartanburghistory.org/walnut-grove-plantation

Sprechen Sie Deutsch?

As an Ulster Scot, Charles Moore immigrated to the British North American colonies during the mid-eighteenth century from Ireland. Also referred to as Scotch Irish, the Ulster Scots were an English-speaking, Germanic, Protestant people. The first records of Moore appear in April of 1752 in Anson County, North Carolina. Ten years later, Moore bought 1,000 acres from Roger Lawson on December 23, 1762. Between 1763 and 1784 he would acquire eight land grants totaling 2,600 acres, not including the acres purchased from Lawson.

He and wife Mary Barry, born circa 1733, had ten children: Margaret, Rachel, Violet, Thomas, Alice, Mary, Rosanna, Elizabeth, Andrew, and Charles Jr. Their son, Thomas, participated in the local militia during the American Revolution.

According to the US Census, Charles owned nine slaves and increased that number to twelve in 1800. In his 1798 will, Moore named eleven slaves. Additionally, there are references to the children of those enslaved people. However, upon his death in 1805, it turned out he had amended his will naming nine slaves instead. A value of $2,650 was given to those slaves mentioned, roughly about $294 each. Present-day archaeological excavations are ongoing in an attempt to learn more about the men, women, and children who once worked Moore's land.

The manor house currently standing is known as a Piedmont farmhouse, which is a classic example of South Carolina backcountry architecture during the 1700s. However, the structure has been altered due to a fire during the 1970s.

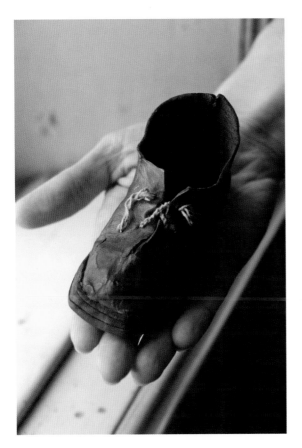

After Charles and Mary both died in 1805, Charles Jr. and his wife Jane Barry lived in the house with their six children until 1826. Thirty years later, from 1856 to 1879, Margaret Anna Moore, the daughter of Charles Moore Sr.'s second son, Dr. Andrew Barry Moore, and her husband Samuel lived in the house. After that, various occupants unrelated to the Moores resided in the house until 1961, when Thomas Moore Craig, fifth generation of Charles Moore, donated the home along with eight acres to the Spartanburg County Historical Association. Today the Piedmont farmhouse has been restored to what it may have looked like in the early nineteenth century.

Woodburn Historic House

130 History Ln.
Pendleton, SC 29670
pendletonhistoricfoundation.org

A Part of the Pinckney Legacy

Son of American Revolutionary War General Thomas Pinckney, Charles Cotesworth Pinckney was born in 1789. He studied to become a lawyer but decided to manage his father's plantation as well as his own, called Woodburn. Charles however did serve in the public forum as the lieutenant governor of South Carolina in 1832.

David S. Taylor was the next owner of the farm; however, not much is known about him. Taylor sold the plantation to Presbyterian minister John Bailey Adger in 1852. Adger's brother Robert

Adger owned Ashtabula Plantation. Keeping the Woodburn property in the family, John Adger later sold it to his other brother Joseph Ellison Adger in 1858.

A nephew of the Adger brothers, Augustine T. Smythe, purchased the property twenty-three years later. Using the property to raise horses and purebred cattle, Smythe also practiced law and was elected three times to the state legislature.

In 1911 William Frederick Calhoun Owen bought Woodburn from Smythe for $20,000. Living on-site until the Great Depression, Owen was forced to foreclose and the South Carolina State Bank of Greenville took over until they could locate another buyer.

That buyer was John Frank. Frank turned the plantation into Woodburn Farms, Inc. on August 15, 1930. Woodburn would not remain in his hands for long, however, as the US government bought the property from him after the Great Depression due to the prevalent challenges experienced throughout the local economy.

During the 1950s, the federal government gave Woodburn Plantation to Clemson College, who in turn gave it to the Pendleton Historic Foundation in 1966. Five years later, in 1971, Woodburn Plantation was listed on the National Register of Historic Places and restored to its present condition. It opened to the public in the 1980s.

Often overshadowed in the property's history is the life of Jane Edna Harris Hunter who was born to a sharecropper family at Woodburn on December 13, 1882. Graduating from Hampton Institute in Virginia in 1905, she went on to become a nurse. Moving to Cleveland, she founded the Working Girls Association in 1911, a boardinghouse for unmarried women living in the city. Because the name implied negative connotations, it was later changed to the Phillis Wheatley Association, after the first female African-American poet published in the United States. The life of this phenomenal woman can be read in her autobiography *A Nickel and a Prayer*.

Open on Sunday to the public, the historic home offers a tour of both floors, its attic, and raised basement. Additionally, on-site nearby is a carriage house and two slave cabin replicas, one dedicated to Mrs. Jane Edna Harris Hunter.

Tourism Boards

Aiken, visitaikensc.com

Beaufort, beaufortsc.org

Camden, classicallycarolina.com

Charleston, charlestoncvb.com

Clemson, visitclemson.com

Columbia, experiencecolumbiasc.com

Discover South Carolina, discoversouthcarolina.com

Florence, visitflo.com

Georgetown, historicgeorgetownsc.com

Greenville, visitgreenvillesc.com

Low Country, southcarolinalowcountry.com

Spartanburg, visitspartanburg.com

Upcountry, upcountrysc.com

Trails

Find Your Park, findyourpark.com

Gullah/Geechee Cultural Heritage Corridor, nps.gov/guge/index.htm

South Carolina's Revolutionary Rivers, visitflo.com/revolutionary-rivers

Index

About the Author

JAI WILLIAMS is an author as well as a travel and culinary photographer. Her photography is visible in digital publications such as the *Washington Post, Anthony Bourdain: Parts Unknown, Serious Eats,* and the Library of Congress to name a few. Her previous co-authored book *Plantations of Virginia* continues to appeal to history and travel aficionados alike.